CLOSE ENCOUNTERS OF THE JESUS KIND
Studies in Luke

TOGETHER IN FAITH SERIES
Leader Session Guide

Brent Christianson

CLOSE ENCOUNTERS OF THE JESUS KIND: STUDIES IN LUKE
Leader Session Guide

Together in Faith Series
Book of Faith Adult Bible Studies

Copyright © 2010 Augsburg Fortress. All rights reserved. Except for brief quotations in critical articles or reviews, no part of this book may be reproduced in any manner without prior written permission from the publisher. For more information, visit: www.augsburgfortress.org/copyrights or write to: Permissions, Augsburg Fortress, Box 1209, Minneapolis, MN 55440-1209.

 Book of Faith is an initiative of the
Evangelical Lutheran Church in America
God's work. Our hands.

For more information about the Book of Faith initiative, go to www.bookoffaith.org.

Scripture quotations, unless otherwise marked, are from New Revised Standard Version Bible, copyright © 1989 Division of Christian Education of the National Council of Churches of Christ in the United States of America. Used by permission. All rights reserved.

Web site addresses are provided in this resource for your use. These listings do not represent an endorsement of the sites by Augsburg Fortress, nor do we vouch for their content for the life of this resource.

ISBN: 978-0-8066-9774-1
Writer: Brent Christianson
Cover and interior design: Spunk Design Machine, spkdm.com
Typesetting: PerfecType, Nashville, TN

The paper used in this publication meets the minimum requirements of American National Standard for Information Sciences—Permanence of Paper for Printed Library Materials, ANSI Z329.48-1984.

Manufactured in the U.S.A.
14 13 12 11 10   1 2 3 4 5 6 7 8 9 10

CONTENTS

Introduction	5
1 Jesus Is Close to Those Estranged by Grief *Luke 7:11-17* (Year C—Lectionary 10)	9
2 Jesus Is Close to Those Estranged by Resentment *Luke 7:36—8:3* (Year C—Lectionary 11)	19
3 Jesus Is Close to Those Estranged by Fear *Luke 8:26-39* (Year C—Lectionary 12)	29
4 Jesus Is Close to Those Estranged by God's Distance *Luke 9:51-62* (Year C—Lectionary 13)	39
5 Jesus Is Close to Those Seeking the Estranged *Luke 10:1-11, 16-20* (Year C—Lectionary 14)	49
6 Jesus Is Close to Those Learning from the Estranged *Luke 10:25-37* (Year C—Lectionary 15)	59

Introduction

Book of Faith Adult Bible Studies

Welcome to the conversation! The Bible study resources you are using are created to support the bold vision of the Book of Faith initiative that calls "the whole church to become more fluent in the first language of faith, the language of Scripture, in order that we might live into our calling as a people renewed, enlivened, empowered, and sent by the Word."

Simply put, this initiative and these resources invite you to "Open Scripture. Join the Conversation."

We enter into this conversation based on the promise that exploring the Bible deeply with others opens us to God working in and through us. God's Word is life changing, church changing, and world changing. Lutheran approaches to Scripture provide a fruitful foundation for connecting Bible, life, and faith.

A Session Overview

Each session is divided into the following four key sections. The amount of time spent in each section may vary based on choices you make. The core Learner Session Guide is designed for 50 minutes. A session can be expanded to as much as 90 minutes by using the Bonus Activities that appear in the Leader Session Guide.

- **Gather (10-15 minutes)**
Time to check in, make introductions, review homework assignments, share an opening prayer, and use the Focus Activity to introduce learners to the Session Focus.

- **Open Scripture (10-15 minutes)**
The session Scripture text is read using a variety of methods and activities. Learners are asked to respond to a few general questions. As leader, you may want to capture initial thoughts or questions on paper for later review.

- **Join the Conversation (25-55 minutes)**
Learners explore the session Scripture text through core questions and activities that cover each of the four perspectives (see diagram on p. 6). The core Learner Session Guide material may be expanded through use of the Bonus Activities provided in the Leader Session Guide. Each session ends with a brief Wrap-up and prayer.

- **Extending the Conversation (5 minutes)**
Lists homework assignments, including next week's session Scripture text. The leader may choose one or more items to assign for all. Each session also includes additional Enrichment options and may include For Further Reading suggestions.

A Method to Guide the Conversation

Book of Faith Adult Bible Studies has three primary goals:

- To increase biblical fluency;
- To encourage and facilitate informed small group conversation based on God's Word; and
- To renew and empower us to carry out God's mission for the sake of the world.

To accomplish these goals, each session will explore one or more primary Bible texts from four different angles and contexts—historical, literary, Lutheran, and devotional. These particular ways of exploring a text are not new, but used in combination they provide a full understanding of and experience with the text.

Complementing this approach is a commitment to engaging participants in active, learner-orientated Bible conversations. The resources call for prepared leaders to facilitate learner discovery, discussion, and activity. Active learning and frequent engagement with Scripture will lead to greater biblical fluency and encourage active faith.

1 We begin by reading the Bible text and reflecting on its meaning. We ask questions and identify items that are unclear. We bring our unique background and experience to the Bible, and the Bible meets us where we are.

5 We return to where we started, but now we have explored and experienced the Bible text from four different dimensions. We are ready to move into the "for" dimension. We have opened Scripture and joined in conversation for a purpose. We consider the meaning of the text for faithful living. We wonder what God is calling us (individually and as communities of faith) to do. We consider how God's Word is calling us to do God's work in the world.

2* We seek to understand the world of the Bible and locate the setting of the text. We explore who may have written the text and why. We seek to understand the particular social and cultural contexts that influenced the content and the message. We wonder who the original audience may have been. We think about how these things "translate" to our world today.

Devotional Context

Historical Context

Lutheran Context

Literary Context

4 We consider the Lutheran principles that help ground our interpretation of the Bible text. We ask questions that bring those principles and unique Lutheran theological insights into conversation with the text. We discover how our Lutheran insights can ground and focus our understanding and shape our faithful response to the text.

3* We pay close attention to how the text is written. We notice what kind of literature it is and how this type of literature may function or may be used. We look at the characters, the story line, and the themes. We compare and contrast these with our own understanding and experience of life. In this interchange, we discover meaning.

> * Sessions may begin with either Historical Context or Literary Context.

The diagram on p. 6 summarizes the general way this method is intended to work. A more detailed introduction to the method used in Book of Faith Adult Bible Studies is available in *Opening the Book of Faith* (Augsburg Fortress, 2008).

The Learner Session Guide

The Learner Session Guide content is built on the four sections (see p. 5). The content included in the main "Join the Conversation" section is considered to be the core material needed to explore the session Scripture text. Each session includes a Focus Image that is used as part of an activity or question somewhere within the core session. Other visuals (maps, charts, photographs, and illustrations) may be included to help enhance the learner's experience with the text and its key concepts.

The Leader Session Guide

For easy reference, the Leader Session Guide contains all the content included in the Learner Session Guide and more. The elements that are unique to the Leader Session Guide are the following:

- **Before You Begin**—Helpful tips to use as you prepare to lead the session.
- **Session Overview**—Contains detailed description of key themes and content covered in each of the four contexts (Historical, Literary, Lutheran, Devotional). Core questions and activities in the Learner Session Guide are intended to emerge directly from this Session Overview. Highlighted parts of the Session Overview provide a kind of "quick prep" for those wanting to do an initial scan of the key session themes and content.
- **Key Definitions**—Key terms or concepts that appear in the Session Overview may be illustrated or defined.
- **Facilitator's Prayer**—To help the leader center on the session theme and leadership task.
- **Bonus Activities**—Optional activities included in each of the four sections of "Join the Conversation" used by the leader to expand the core session.
- **Tips**—A variety of helpful hints, instructions, or background content to aid leadership facilitation.
- **Looking Ahead**—Reminders to the leader about preparation for the upcoming session.

Session Prep Video

(Available on the DVD that accompanies this unit.) To help you prepare to lead the session, Session Prep Video segments have been created. A guide will walk with you through a session overview and the key parts of the session flow. These segments can provide helpful hints, but they are not meant to replace your own deeper preparation.

Leader and Learner

In Book of Faith Adult Bible Studies, the leader's primary task is facilitating small group conversation and activity. These conversations are built around structured learning tasks. What is a structured learning task? It is an open question or activity that engages learners with new content and the resources they need to respond. Underlying this structured dialog approach are three primary assumptions about adult learners:

- Adult learners bring with them varied experiences and the capability to do active learning tasks;
- Adult learners learn best when they are invited to be actively involved in learning; and
- Adults are more accountable and engaged when active learning tasks are used.

Simply put, the goal is fluency in the first language of faith, the language of Scripture. How does one become fluent in a new language, proficient in building houses, or skilled at hitting a baseball? By practicing and doing in a hands-on way. Book of Faith Adult Bible Studies provides the kind of hands-on Bible exploration that will produce Bible-fluent learners equipped to do God's work in the world.

Together in Faith Series

Throughout its history, the church has established lists of Scripture readings appropriate for each Sunday and festival day of the church year calendar. These lists, called lectionaries, identify the Scripture readings used for worship in many congregations. While a lectionary-guided connection with the Bible typically occurs in the context of corporate worship, the thematic approach of Together in Faith can link the gathering of small groups around the Book of Faith with the congregation's gathering around the Word in worship. Online worship helps are provided so that preachers and worship planners can create congregation-wide experiences around each of the Together in Faith units. The flexibility of the Together in Faith online helps makes the units useful for any time of the year. The small group session materials are also designed to serve as stand-alone studies for anytime use.

Close Encounters of the Jesus Kind: Studies in Luke Unit Overview

All of the Gospel writers—indeed, all of Scripture—tell how God chooses to break the power of what separates us from God in order to bring us into a relationship of faith. Faith is trust built on love. Luke, more than the other evangelists, emphasizes God's loving choice in Christ to befriend those who are estranged and considered outsiders. His close encounters with sinners, foreigners, those who were unclean, those who were young, women, tax collectors, prostitutes, those who were poor, and others reveal the inclusivity of grace.

We can all become strangers and, as the 1960s song by The Doors, "People are Strange," reminds us, everything gets distorted in our alienation. Estrangement distorts life for all involved. God's desire in Christ is to free us from those things that keep us from seeing God and God's creation in clear and hopeful ways. These close encounters in Luke's Gospel tell of how Christ engaged the estranged of Luke's time and speak to us of how he does the same for us now.

Session 1: Jesus Is Close to Those Estranged by Grief (Luke 7:11-17)

How many ways do we experience death? How many ways can we enter life? Jesus says "no" to death and "yes" to life.

Session 2: Jesus Is Close to Those Estranged by Resentment (Luke 7:36—8:3)

Who are people we might resent? Who might resent us? Both main characters here are alienated—the woman by her reputation and the Pharisee by his need to preserve a reputation. Jesus says "no" to the separation of sin and "yes" to the healing of forgiveness.

Session 3: Jesus Is Close to Those Estranged by Fear (Luke 8:26-39)

How can fear make us crazy? The legion of demons in the Gerasene feared Jesus; his people feared him in his insanity and in his sanity, and they feared Jesus' power. Jesus says "no" to fear and "yes" to freedom.

Session 4: Jesus Is Close to Those Estranged by God's Distance (Luke 9:51-62)

How do we experience the distance or nearness of God? Here, strangely, Jesus is revealed as the outsider, choosing to move with determination to Jerusalem and reveal a God who is not distant but always present. Jesus says "no" to an excluded God and has become the "yes" of God with us.

Session 5: Jesus Is Close to Those Seeking the Estranged (Luke 10:1-11, 16-20)

What are the important invitations we have received and given? In this text, Jesus sends out his followers to call all people to enter into the new day of God. Jesus says "no" to in-groups and "yes" to community.

Session 6: Jesus Is Close to Those Learning from the Estranged (Luke 10:25-37)

How have painful experiences actually helped you become a more gracious person? This famous parable tells how it may be our recognition of our own experience of alienation and exclusion, when touched by God's mercy, which helps us reach out to others.

SESSION ONE

Luke 7:11-17

Leader Session Guide

Focus Statement

Death takes many forms, but God in Christ restores us to live joyfully and hopefully in communion with God, creation, and the human family.

Key Verse

The dead man sat up and began to speak, and Jesus gave him to his mother. Luke 7:15

Focus Image

A very fresh grave. © Javier Kohen. Used under Creative Commons 3.0 License.

Jesus Is Close to Those Estranged by Grief

Session Preparation

Before You Begin...

This session deals with death and resurrection. You or learners in your group may have had recent encounters with the death of a loved one. Be sensitive to the tendency to say Jesus takes away the pain of death. Christians do and should grieve, Paul says, but we are not without hope (1 Thessalonians 4:13).

Session Instructions

1. Read this Session Guide completely and highlight or underline any portions you wish to emphasize with the group. Note any Bonus Activities you wish to do.

2. If you plan to do any special activities, check to see what materials you'll need, if any.

3. Have extra Bibles on hand in case a member of the group forgets to bring one.

4. Please note that one of the devotional options for initial reading of the session text requires the use of a candle. Before lighting candles, check your local fire codes and your congregation's fire polices regarding the use of open flames.

Session Overview

In conversations about Jesus raising the dead son of the widow of Nain, you will help each other understand that beyond God's promise of resurrection at the last day, Christians have God's presence to touch us by grace in all those ways we encounter death in our daily lives. God does this in order to keep restoring us to life and community, where our presence and service are needed by others.

HISTORICAL CONTEXT

Jesus breaks a couple of formal and informal rules here. First, he interrupts a funeral procession. How would we feel about that? Then he touches a dead man—only the closest of relatives could do so without becoming ritually unclean (Leviticus 21:1-3; Numbers 19:11). Jesus shows that no barriers—not ritual laws, or societal norms, or even death—will stand in the way of God's **compassion**. Jesus also shows how God regards our concepts of purity and impurity.

SESSION ONE

 Compassion:

"He had compassion on her" (Luke 7:13). The original Greek word is not only interesting, but is very significant in Luke and it's fun to say! *Splangchnizomai* (*splangk-NIZ-o-mai*—you'll have to practice that!) comes from the word *splangchnon*, which means, well, guts. It describes a feeling of compassion that is incarnational and physical. In addition to the session text, it is used to describe the feeling of the good Samaritan (Luke 10:34) and the father of the prodigal son (Luke 15:20). God's compassion for the lost is described in physical and human terms. God in Christ would have it no other way.

People who lived in the time of Christ's ministry might look at the modern treatment of death and funeral practices and ask why dying is so private and emotionally sanitized (in hospitals, away from family and community). They might wonder why we try to make the dead person look not dead. There is much about our society that is "death denying" in an unhealthy way. Your group may want to talk about the differences in funeral practices between that time and our own and see how their public mourning and community acknowledgement of grief might be healthier than our own practices.

In Jesus' day, the death of a widow's only son meant complete poverty and helplessness. Jesus' compassion certainly was for the widow—but the dead man certainly benefited as well! Jesus' compassion touched all who were there, but in ways particular to the needs of each person.

Literary Context

The style here is straightforward prose—no poetry, no metaphor, no hidden meanings. The significance of who Jesus is and what God is doing through him are the underlying themes of this account. The Sermon on the Plain (Luke 6:17-49) gives a plain view of Jesus' emphasis on seeking and including the outsider and the excluded. Immediately before our session text in Luke 7, we encounter the story of a Roman centurion who intercedes for his slave, and Jesus grants healing. In the session text, Jesus finds people who are "outsiders"—the dead man, outside life; the widow, outside hope; the crowds, outside the city. There is drama in the action—the procession stops; the Lord reaches out to touch the dead body; the dead man is no longer dead but alive and given by Jesus back to his mother. The words from Jesus' Sermon on the Plain about the mourners' tears turning to laughter come true in our session text.

This account of resurrection is also a way of looking forward to the resurrection of another "only son"—Jesus. The hearers in the early church would have made the connection. Participants might be asked if the language here reminds them of other accounts in the Bible—you may need to prod them with the words *only son* and *resurrection*.

Lutheran Context

The Lutheran understanding of law and gospel is very helpful at this point in the session. You will be dealing with elements that might challenge, accuse, and even condemn us, which is the function of the law as we are reminded in passages such as Romans 7:21-25 and 1 Corinthians 15:56-58. We are reminded by Luke 7:11-17 that life itself can address us as "law." There are events in our lives that are "deaths"—endings, sorrows, terminations, failures, and so on—that can also speak words of accusation and condemnation. However, Jesus speaks a different word. The gospel speaks to us in our "deaths" with words of hope and divine presence.

With this in mind, learners are asked to consider those aspects of their life that strike them as "law"—accusation and condemnation. Keep in mind that sometimes these are needed. An alcoholic, for instance, might hear the admonishment not to drink as accusation, but it is needed nonetheless. Luther's advice is to hear Christ's action or word in Luke as an invitation to positively consider the accusing voice of the law. To feel Christ's touch is to be freed from that condemnation, to correct the error (stop drinking!), and to move on to live in community.

Lutheran theology proclaims that we are freed from the requirements of the law not simply to go our own way but that our work might be not for our salvation but for the good of our neighbor. God has looked with **favor** upon us and on others through us! Passages like 2 Corinthians 3:1-6 remind us that God has made us "letters of Christ" who have both the calling and the competence to be a "word of life" (1 John 1:1-4) to others.

 Favor:
"God has looked favorably on his people!" (Luke 7:16b). The verb used here also can mean "visit"—God is not simply watching but is a part of the activity of God's people—here the mourners.

Devotional Context

This text is full of the deep "stuff" of human life: community, separation, family units and family disintegration, the needs of culture, and the requirements of living as human beings. It presents the ultimate themes of Christian faith: life and death, God's presence in sorrow, the promised resurrection, and the reality of fear and wonder.

The challenge of the devotional reading is to move these deep things into the experienced reality of the participants' lives. The theme of this session is looking for how God restores us to life. In this story, Jesus not only restores the dead youth to life but restores a family, touches a community of mourners, and, perhaps, changes how all look at the connections we have with each other.

"Death" has many meanings. Of course, at the end of our life, we die. But we all know the pain or ambiguity of endings and

SESSION ONE

failures and disappointments. A devotional reading of this text allows us to acknowledge the reality of death in all its dimensions and to ask Christ to touch us in those places to restore us to life and community. Learners are encouraged to think about the ways we experience death and how God touches us there.

Facilitator's Prayer

Dear God, you have entrusted me to be part of a people journeying through your word. Guide me as I seek to guide; lead me as I seek to lead; be gracious to me that I might be gracious and hold all of us in your merciful compassion. Amen.

Gather (10-15 minutes)

Check-in

Take this time to connect or reconnect with the others in your group. Talk about a time when you felt you "really belonged" to a group or community. What was the community and what did belonging to it feel like?

Pray

Dear God, so often we find ourselves outside of community, lifeless, grieving our losses, and confronting death. In Christ you faced death. You returned in resurrection. Bless us with the promise of resurrection and help that promise to form our daily lives. In Jesus' name. Amen.

Focus Activity

Take time to look at and talk about the Focus Image. Share what you think might be the story behind the fresh grave. Share similar sights you have seen in person. How does looking at the picture make you feel? The picture is of something literal and "real," but are there also some symbolic meanings of the picture? What else might the picture symbolize?

Tip:
The photograph of a fresh grave may bring up memories of graves learners have encountered and, perhaps, grief or the fear of dying. It may be that some recognize an open grave not merely as one waiting to receive a body, but one that has, on the last day, been opened for entry into a life that will not end. You may want to suggest that neither option robs the other of its emotional and life-changing power. Death still hurts, but it does not deny resurrection.

SESSION ONE

Open Scripture (10-15 minutes)

After reading the scripture once, have learners break into the characters of the reading. Have the youngest "play" Jesus and the oldest play the dead youth.

Turn out the lights. Take time for silence. Light a candle and read the text. Leave time for silence before turning the lights back on.

Read Luke 7:11-17.
- Talk about the characters in the text. Which ones can you most and least relate to?
- What emotions stand out in this text for you? Who is feeling them? Which ones make the most sense to you?
- What changes at the end of the text and what remains the same?

Join the Conversation (25-55 minutes)

Historical Context

To this day in the Middle East, burial on the same day of death is the norm. In Jesus' day, burials were always outside of populated areas—cities, towns, villages. Friends of the deceased participated in the funeral, as well as official mourners who accompanied the body. Contact with a dead body made the one who touched it ritually unclean. There were no "safety nets" for the poor in Jesus' time. Both the mourners present and those who heard the story would know that a childless widow faced absolute poverty.

1. The raising of a widow's son is only found in Luke's Gospel. In this brief but significant passage, Jesus breaks a number of formal and informal rules.
- Informally speaking, what about this story might be considered to be rude or even cruel?
- Formally speaking, how do Jesus' actions compare with Leviticus 21:1-3 and Numbers 19:11?

2. Why do you think Jesus was so willing to break these social and theological rules? Compare Jesus' actions in Luke 7:11-17 with Luke 9:59-60. How does this comparison enhance our understanding of Jesus' motivations?

 Bonus Activity:
"Fear seized all of them" (Luke 7:16a). The "fear" mentioned here appears to be a good thing. In what ways might this be so? Why is fear often thought of as a bad thing in our time?

Session 1: Luke 7:11-17

SESSION ONE

Tip:
Use whiteboard or chart paper to have learners list as many modern funeral practices as they can. Discuss what practices we consider to be the most important and which would disturb us if they were interrupted or stopped. Compare these feelings to Jesus' "interruption" of this funeral procession in Luke 7.

Bonus Activity:
Are participants familiar with burial practices in other cultures and religions? Discuss why these rituals might be important.

Tip:
Have the group briefly scan Luke 7 for evidence of Jesus' compassion for the estranged—those trapped and struggling on the outskirts of acceptance.

Tip:
There is drama in this story—the pathos of a death, the confrontation of Jesus with death, and the restoration of life. Help participants sense the drama by recording all the learners' sets of five words—in order, verse by verse—and then have them read/act out just those words in a reader's theater fashion. Take note of ways to share what you are discussing and doing in your small group in the congregational worship setting.

Bonus Activity:
Identify the various characters in the text. Place them along a line on the floor, and invite participants to stand near the characters they most closely relate to.

Bonus Activity:
If someone you loved were to be given back to you from death, what are some things you would say to or do with him or her?

3. As a group, make a list of the five most significant rituals or acts that take place in the context of Christian funerals. Discuss how disruption of each would make us feel. Can you imagine Jesus interrupting those rituals or acts in some way? What might be his intention for doing so?

Literary Context

Jesus has been opening the word of God through his ministry in Galilee. In the previous chapter (Luke 6), he preaches the Sermon on the Plain, which is much like and much different from Matthew's account of the Sermon on the Mount (Matthew 5). Especially in Luke's version of the Beatitudes, the emphasis is on blessing for those who are outcast and weak and woe for those who are "insiders" and strong (Luke 6:20-26). Immediately after this sermon, Jesus heals the servant of a Roman centurion (sort of a double-outsider!), and then Jesus meets this funeral procession—outside the city, outside society, outside hope.

1. How do the events of Luke 7 fulfill Jesus' words of blessing in Luke 6:20-21?

2. Reread Luke 7:11-17 silently. Chose *no more than* five words—consecutive or standing alone—that convey the drama of this moment to you. What sorts of events have similar drama in modern times?

In the raising of the widow's son, Jesus is moved deeply by the scene. The Greek word for *compassion* in the original text means literally to "feel in one's gut." Jesus' reaction is prompted by the widow's loss of family and support.

3. Write a list of 10 possessions and relationships you consider most important. Begin crossing them out one by one. At what point do you "feel in your gut" the pain of loss? Share your findings. How do the words *only son* (Luke 7:12) connect to the great pain described in Luke 23:44-48 and 1 John 4:9-11? What is the even greater blessing that came out of these moments?

Lutheran Context

When Lutherans speak of the law, we are not only speaking of specific words that accuse and condemn us, but also of the events of life that can trap and imprison us. The reality of death is painful, and the revelation of God's love in Christ's willingness to die on the cross shows us that in those places where the accusing voice of the law imprisons us, Christ is active.

1. Read Romans 7:21-25. As a group, develop a list of the ways the accusing voice of the law is heard in our daily life. How can this be understood as a struggle with a "body of death"?

2. Read 1 Corinthians 15:56-58. What functions as gospel both here and in our session text, giving life and freeing from sin and death?

Luther's advice is that when we read of Christ saying or doing anything in the Gospels, we should know that he is saying or doing these things to us. He touches people living the real effects of the law and brings life. As Jesus gives the man back to his mother and back into community to live life, we believe that we are freed from the accusation of the law so that we might live for our neighbor.

3. Share specific ways you have seen Christ "touch" those who were previously touched by sin, death, or the accusing voice of the law. How does 2 Corinthians 3:1-6 relate to our role in this ministry of life?

Devotional Context

As you read and listen to this story of Jesus, what are the feelings and thoughts and memories that come to you? There are many in the text—sorrow and mourning, anxiety about the future, compassion felt in the "gut," perhaps the offense of some in the crowd at Jesus' stopping the rite, the utter amazement of the witnesses of the resurrection, awe and fear and glory.

1. Look at the text and underline those feelings that speak to you most.

2. Think about the ways that death in all its dimensions has touched you and people you know. As you hear of Jesus touching the dead man, share the ways he is touching you to restore you to life. Also share the words that you believe describe this life in Christ—include physical and non-physical aspects (such as emotions and spirituality) as well as individual and community aspects.

3. Take time for meditative prayer. Don't be afraid to acknowledge where grief and death are touching you. Ask Jesus to touch you and return you to life.

Tip:
Remember that law does not mean "bad" to the gospel's "good." We often need the corrective voice of the law. It becomes "bad" when it controls our life. The Lutheran emphasis is not to free us from works but rather to free our works from being for our salvation emphasizing instead that they're for the

Bonus Activity:
Make a list of ways daily life can address us as "law." Discuss how or whether these are corrective or how the voice of the law can be controlling.

Bonus Activity:
Read 1 John 1:1-4. The writer was clearly "touched" by the "word of life" that Jesus offered. What blessings of this "word of life" are evident in this passage? Make a list of how we need community ("fellowship") and how our various communities need us.

Tip:
Challenge the group to think of death in other forms besides the physical passing away. What other kinds of death do we experience in life?

Bonus Activity:
Invite participants to write a prayer for God's restoration into life for their week ahead, and encourage them to pray it daily.

SESSION ONE

Tip:
You may wish to read the following from Nikos Kazantzakis's book, *Report to Greko*. Writing about a monk showing young tourists the tomb he has carved out for himself, he says: "'Look at what I've carved on it,' he shouted at us, 'Bend down, then, don't be afraid, I tell you, and read it.' He knelt down, brushed the dirt off the carved letters, and read out: 'Hey, I'm not afraid of you, Death!' He looked at us, and even his ears shook with laughter. 'Why should I be afraid of the rascal? He's just a mule, I'll climb on his back and he will take me to God.'" (Nikos Kazantzakis, *Report to Greco*, New York: Simon and Schuster, 1965)

Tip:
You may want to ask participants to name those whom they loved who have died and with whom they will share in resurrection.

Wrap-up

1. If there are any questions to explore further, write them on a whiteboard or chart paper. Ask for volunteers to do research to share with the group at the next session.

2. Learners may wish to discuss whether it is easy or difficult for us to talk about death today. Should our Christian faith make a difference in such discussion?

3. Where have participants witnessed God's activity of restoring someone to life?

4. Encourage group members to go online to www.bookoffaith.org to learn more about this Bible fluency initiative.

Pray

Gracious God, in Christ, you bring us out of death and into life. Be with us in the days ahead and give us faith to hear your voice and grace to share your life. In Jesus' name. Amen.

Extending the Conversation (5 minutes)

Homework

1. Read the next session's Bible text: Luke 7:36—8:3.

2. In our day it is easy for most of us to think that the time for mourning is done once the funeral is over. But any of us who have lost one to death knows that isn't true. Do you know of someone who has lost a loved one to death within the last year? Renew your concern for that person. Pray for and then call this person to let him or her know of your love and concern.

3. Think of the ways God has restored you to life. Make a list and thank God for God's mercy.

4. What are ways you sense you need restoring to life and community? It might be a wounded friendship or a decrease in a favorite activity with others. Seek God's help to restore those things or relationships.

5. Reach out and touch someone with an invitation to join your Book of Faith conversation with the Gospel of Luke. It's never too late to share the word of life!

Enrichment

1. There are reasons for the kinds of mourning rituals people have. If you have access to the Internet, look up the practices of various religions and societies. Sites like www.myfunkyfuneral.com can offer some unique stories. Bring some of your findings to share with the group.

2. Look at the funeral liturgy in *Evangelical Lutheran Worship* (pp. 279-285). Why is the service structured as it is and why are elements included? You may want to speak to your pastor about this.

3. Check out www.bookoffaith.org to learn more about this Bible fluency initiative. Start a group homepage or get involved with the other social networking you can find there.

For Further Reading

The Stewardship of Life in the Kingdom of Death by Douglas John Hall (Grand Rapids: Eerdmans, 1988). Powerful and simple meditations on the ways Christians can respond to a world that has made a "covenant with death" by proclaiming God's covenant of life.

Available from augsburgfortress.org/store:

Good Grief by Granger Westberg (Minneapolis: Augsburg Books, 2004). A classic and easily read work on the necessity of facing and working through the grief we experience in the course of human life.

Grievers Ask: Answers to Questions about Death and Loss by Harold Ivan Smith (Minneapolis: Augsburg Books, 2004). Smith compiles more than 150 common questions, explores the emotions behind them, and provides clear and forthright responses.

Looking Ahead

1. Read the next session's Bible text: Luke 7:36—8:3.

2. Read through the Leader Guide for the next session and mark portions you wish to highlight for the group.

3. Make a checklist of any materials you'll need to do the Bonus Activities.

4. Pray for members of your group during the week.

SESSION TWO

Luke 7:36—8:3

Leader Session Guide

Focus Statement
In a world of contempt, derision, and resentment, the presence of the kingdom of God in Christ Jesus means forgiveness, love, and restoration.

Key Verse
And he said to the woman, "Your faith has saved you; go in peace." Luke 7:50

Focus Image

Who do you think you're talking to? © SuperStock RF / SuperStock

Jesus Is Close to Those Estranged by Resentment

Session Preparation

Before You Begin . . .

The text for this day presents themes of reputation and resentment. The woman and Simon are both prisoners of reputation. Simon is further bound by resenting others—the woman who was a "sinner" and Jesus who wasn't behaving as Simon thought he should. The text deals also with forgiveness—and whether forgiveness is ever "little." All humans harbor fears and resentment and sin; and all humans are invited into God's new day of freedom and forgiveness. Pray that you and all in the study group will better understand (and stand under!) freedom and forgiveness by the end of the session.

Session Instructions

1. Read this Session Guide completely and highlight or underline any portions you wish to emphasize with the group. Note any Bonus Activities you wish to do.

2. If you plan to do any special activities, check to see what materials you'll need, if any.

3. Have extra Bibles on hand in case a member of the group forgets to bring one.

4. Have on hand either a whiteboard or newsprint to record responses of the group.

Session Overview

This session will allow us to look at our own tendencies to judge others or be too protective of ourselves—raising walls of resentment and isolation. Our session text moves us to reconsider those tendencies in the light of God's will to forgive and break down the barriers that we build.

HISTORICAL CONTEXT

Jesus is sharing a meal with Simon the Pharisee who has invited him to his home—a sign of respect and honor in Jesus' time. Pharisees were one of several denominations in first-century Judaism. They were among the few Jewish groups strong enough to survive the fall of Jerusalem in 70 C.E. While the Pharisees are often presented in the New Testament as a bit of a caricature,

SESSION TWO

Pharisee:
There is no unanimous agreement about the name. It could come from the word for "separate" (*par-USH*), indicating their desire for purity in obeying Torah. It could come from the word for "interpreting" scripture (*par-ASH*) for their zeal in the study of scripture. And some propose it was a label applied by the Sadducees referring to them as "Persians" who brought into Judaism such foreign ideas as the resurrection of the dead, which entered Jewish spirituality after the Babylonian captivity.

a legalistic foil to Jesus, this is more of a literary device than a historically accurate view. The voice they represent in the Gospels—that of constricted legalists—is found in all societies. E. P. Sanders, one of the finest scholars of first-century Judaism, writes this about the Pharisees:

> I rather like the Pharisees. They loved detail and precision. They wanted to get everything just right. I like that. They loved God, they thought he had blessed them, and they thought that God wanted them to get everything just right. I do not doubt that some of them were priggish. This is a common fault of the pious, one that is amply displayed in modern criticism of the Pharisees. The Pharisees, we know, intended to be humble before God, and they thought that intention mattered more than outward show. Those are worthy ideals. (*Judaism: Practice and Belief 63 B.C.E.–66 C.E.* [Philadelphia: SCM Press, 1992], p. 494)

LITERARY CONTEXT

The greater section of Luke that contains this text (Luke 3:1—9:50) presents the person, the message, and the mission of Jesus. His ancestry, the baptism by John, temptation, calling the disciples, teaching, and healing in Galilee join in revealing him to his people and to the reader of Luke as one who teaches with authority and reaches out to those who are thought beyond the boundaries of community and faith. In Luke 7:36—8:3, the evangelist employs three literary forms in service of this goal: first-person narrative, parable, and third-person narrative.

At first we find Jesus in the company of both the insider's insider (a male Pharisee) and an outsider's outsider (a woman who was a "sinner in the city"). As soon as the woman enters the house, the reader knows something significant will happen. The Pharisee is offended. The woman is defended and, in fact, is presented as a better example of faith than the one whom Luke describes as one who knows he is the standard of faith!

Denarius:
A silver Roman coin thought to be the typical daily wage for a common worker.

Jesus then unpacks this emotionally charged moment with a parable. The parable Jesus presents is, at face, hyperbolic and hard to believe. A **denarius** was a day's wage. Both debtors owed a large amount, neither could pay, and both were graciously forgiven. What kind of a banker would do that? Jesus knows the answer; the woman knows the answer; Simon isn't quite there yet. The word Jesus uses for "debtor" here is only used in one other place in Luke—the parable of the "unjust steward" (Luke

16:1-9). Both creditors forgave prodigiously and completely. One may assume the ones who were forgiven didn't question the motive of the forgiver.

Moving into chapter 8, we find Luke using a word in verse 1 that is translated "proclaiming the good news." This is also a word used to describe the announcement of the presence of the empire by the representative of Caesar. Luke's Jesus is presenting an alternate **kingdom**—one based not on military might and conquest but on mercy and forgiveness and healing. The good news here is one of victory over resentment and estrangement.

Lutheran Context

One of the most dangerous practices of religious people is to locate sin and evil "out there" somewhere, that is, in someone else. For this reason, Martin Luther urges us in the explanation to the Eighth Commandment in his Small Catechism to try to explain one another's actions in the kindest way. We can easily locate hypocrisy in Simon the Pharisee and thus miss our own. Simon located sin in the woman and, by extension, in Jesus (who didn't measure up to Simon's standards). Jesus' parable leaves a question that hovers unanswered: Is there ever forgiveness that is "little"?

Sin is sin and always separates us from God. There are actions and thoughts we have that hurt us and others. We need to pay attention to them, but Luther reminded us that "sins" are simply signs that "Sin" is present in the way that the pocks of chicken pox are not the disease but the sign that the virus is there. "Sin" (with a capital "S") is the underlying failure we all have to "fear, love, and trust God above all things." The Pharisee's problem in this text is his confusion of "sins" with "Sin" and his assumption that, since he lacked "sin" he was also fairly safe from "Sin." The parable reminds us that when you can't pay a debt, 50 days' wages is as impossible as 500 days' wages.

When the word addresses us as law, it shows both our "sin" and our "Sin." It does that not to leave us sputtering, but to open us to the gospel proclamation of God's forgiveness of both in Christ. The medieval church saw in the sacramental system a sort of chipping away at the power of "sin." The reformer proclaimed a greater miracle and mystery—in Baptism, forgiveness, and Holy Communion we encounter the living God who completely forgives "Sin" and enlivens the sinner. Sometimes we dance with joy, and sometimes we weep gratefully, and sometimes we simply sleep peacefully.

 Kingdom:
The Roman Empire was the only kingdom recognized in the Mediterranean basin during the first century C.E. Any use of that word challenged Rome. Jesus' use of the term *kingdom of God* does not mean heaven, but the proclamation that God, not Caesar, is in charge.

SESSION TWO

Devotional Context

There is something for everyone in this text. Sometimes we feel worthless and looked down upon—like the woman in the text must have felt. Sometimes we feel superior or resentful like Simon. Sometimes we feel buried in problems like the debtors. Sometimes we feel the power of forgiveness like the woman and the debtors. Sometimes we feel so close to Jesus that we are his companions like the people on the road. Sometimes we feel so far from Jesus that we are like those in the villages not knowing what wonder is coming.

Whatever our situation, feeling, fear, or hope, the same Jesus is with us and for us and bringing the kingdom of God—God's new day of favor (2 Corinthians 6:1-2) into our day-to-day lives. The value of a text such as this is that it can touch us in any number of circumstances and conditions. We are allowed honesty here—we can see ourselves as any of the characters in the text without soft-peddling or euphemism. The good news is that Jesus comes to us, meets us where we are, and goes about the work of forgiveness.

Facilitator's Prayer

Dear God, you are trusting me to be faithful and gracious as I explore your word with brothers and sisters. Give me faith, grace, and trust in your spirit to guide us. Give me love for those I join in the mystery of your word. And open us all to your new day. In Christ. Amen.

Gather (10-15 minutes)

Check-in

Take this time to connect or reconnect with the others in your group. Be ready to share new thoughts or insights about your last session. Share also one of the homework assignments from last week that you found helpful in deepening or expanding your faith life.

Pray

God of amazing love, you have placed us into human communities and called us to love and serve each other. Dear God, we try to do that, but we know we often resent and judge others. Open us to the marvel and mystery of your reign of forgiveness. Help us to hear forgiveness, speak forgiveness, and live in love as you are love. In Jesus' name. Amen.

Tip:
If there are new members in this session, take time for introductions. Invite members to "check-in" with each other, that is, share something significant that happened this week.

Tip:
Invite several seconds of silence before and after the prayer. Ask all to pray it together, encouraging them to speak the prayer just a bit more slowly than normal speech as a way to step back and focus.

22 Close Encounters of the Jesus Kind Leader Guide

SESSION TWO

Focus Activity

Take time to look at the picture and then create a story around the Focus Image. Talk about what happened to lead up to the picture. What actions or words or emotions were taking place? Then discuss what you see in the picture—literally what you see and what you think is happening beneath the surface for the person you see. Then talk about what happens after the picture—create at least two possible outcomes. Were you ever in a similar situation?

Tip:
Write on the whiteboard or chart paper the responses for actions, words, and emotions. Also write the two possible outcomes. Encourage discussion of similar situations some have faced.

Open Scripture (10-15 minutes)

Give each participant paper for drawing and crayons or colored pencils. As one participant reads the text, encourage the others to draw at least one "action shot" of any part of the text.

Tip:
Bring in an aromatic oil or cream of some kind. Open it as the text is being read so that the aroma fills the space. You might want to ask beforehand if any group members have any allergic reactions to such aromas.

Read the text in an NRSV Bible and then find and read it in a children's Bible.

Read Luke 7:36—8:3.

- If you could have taken a picture of one action in this text that would "tell the whole story" what would it be?
- What do the verses in chapter 8 have to do with the verses in chapter 7?
- In what ways does this text speak to the relationship between forgiveness and love?

Join the Conversation (25-55 minutes)

Historical Context

At the time Luke was written, Jerusalem had been destroyed and the Jewish nation was disintegrating. The Pharisees and the followers of Jesus were two of the Jewish groups that survived. Luke mentioned Pharisees as a way of preparing for a confrontation, the likes of which the faithful of his time often had with other Jews. Although often cast as villains, Pharisees were a people in first-century Judaism who deeply loved God. They desired, above all things, to be faithful to God's directives. They also desired to listen and learn from others who were faithful to God.

Tip:
Find a picture of an old silent movie "bad guy" or a picture of Snidely Whiplash from *The Dudley Do-right Show*. Such caricatures are short-handed ways of letting people know an opponent was on the scene. This literary device is similar to the use of Pharisees as a stereotype of a certain kind of attitude rather than a historically accurate picture.

Session 2: Luke 7:36—8:3

SESSION TWO

1. In what ways does Luke 7:36-50 support the Pharisee's desire to be faithful and learn from Jesus?

2. To invite a person to dine, at that time, was to show hospitality and honor. Table fellowship was a sign of trust and openness. What other forms of hospitality are found in today's session text?

3. For all people who seek to be faithful—not only for Pharisees—there often is a tendency to watch out for those who are not faithful and thus might corrupt the seeker. A woman who was a sinner would be such a person. A rabbi who seemed not to recognize just such a sinner would be another, let alone a rabbi who allowed women to be a part of his congregation and accepted their support would also challenge a system of religious self-reliance and male predominance.

- Luke doesn't tell us, but what do you think was the nature of the woman's sin? Do you think the particular sin was important or just that fact that she was known, somehow, to be disreputable?

- What kinds of people make us uncomfortable when they are around us? How does knowing this about ourselves help us to understand the thoughts of the Pharisee in Luke 7:39?

Literary Context

There are three types of literature in this text. First, there is the account of the meal at the Pharisee's house. Then, there is the parable of the two debtors. Finally, the first verses of chapter 8 are transitional verses that provide a summary of Jesus' ministry and his companions.

1. The parable in Luke 7:40-43 clarifies the encounter between Jesus, the Pharisee, and the woman. Both debtors had considerable debt—a denarius was a day's wage.

- Jesus often uses exaggeration to make a point. What kind of manager would so casually cancel a debt? Is the parable only about the money?

- What in the session text speaks to the true value of the ointment? The kind of ointment the woman was putting on Jesus' feet is mentioned once more in Luke. Read Luke 23:56 and list the reasons these two applications of ointment belong together.

2. Luke 8:1-3 helps us understand the economy of grace in the kingdom of God. Luke's readers would understand whenever the term *kingdom* was used—the kingdom they were always hearing about was Rome. Luke even uses language that might be voiced

Bonus Activity:
Read the description of Pharisees by E. P. Sanders from the Session Overview. Invite participants to share observations of people in their own experience who fit Sanders's description.

Tip:
The normal assumption is that the woman's sin was one of a sexual nature. Why is that the case? Challenge participants to think of her situation less in terms of "sin" and more in terms of "Sin."

Bonus Activity:
Invite someone to be an advocate for Simon the Pharisee and try to convince to group that his opinion was the right one.

Tip:
Do the math: what would be the modern equivalent of those debts?

Bonus Activity:
Invite two volunteers to act out the parable—encourage them to add details and exercise creative license. Give them a few minutes to prepare.

by a representative of Rome announcing the presence of Caesar's kingdom.

- Christ, however, is announcing the presence of the "kingdom of God." What kind of news is this? What is it about the characters mentioned in this passage that supports the idea that this is the announcement of a very different kind of kingdom?
- Are there characters in modern literature, the news, sports, or entertainment of whom, when they are introduced, we already know what to expect? Share examples. Is that true of Jesus in this text? Why or why not? How about the Pharisees or the woman? Read 1 Corinthians 5:16-17, then discuss how grace has the power to alter our presuppositions and resentments.

Lutheran Context

A well-meaning Sunday school teacher was heard to say, "We should thank Jesus we're not like those awful Pharisees!" It is precisely because we are all both sinful as Pharisees and sinful as the "woman in the city" that this text can address us as law. Will we, like the woman, acknowledge sin, or will we, like the Pharisee, try to locate it elsewhere?

Bonus Activity:

Brainstorm contemporary phrases that could be given a very different meaning by changing a single word—just as Jesus' use of "kingdom of God" challenged the "kingdom of Caesar." These can be fun, for instance, "Take me out to the ball game" could be changed to "Take me out of the ball game."

1. Read Martin Luther's explanation of the Eighth Commandment from his Small Catechism. Try to explain the Pharisee's actions in the kindest way. How would you explain the woman's actions?

2. The Pharisee in Luke 7:39-43 was locating sin somewhere other than in himself. Where was he looking for sin? Why is this dangerous?

Luther noted that the kinds of "sins" that tend to draw our attention are "puppy sins." They are serious enough, but our concentration on "sins" hides our "Sin" from us. Our "Sin"—with a capital "S"—is the human inability to fear, love, and trust God above all things. I can be satisfied that I'm not an open thief, compared to someone else who might be. But we both share our inability to believe and act as we should.

Tip:

Invite learners to think of situations in which what is obvious is simply a manifestation of what is the underlying reality (like a bad smell in the refrigerator!).

Bonus Activity:

Luther advised that the First Commandment is really the only one we need—if we could keep that we wouldn't need the others. Share the commandment and Luther's explanation as follows and discuss why that could be the case: "You shall have no other gods. *What does this mean?* We are to fear, love, and trust in God above all things" (*ELW*, p. 1160).

3. After a long list of "sins" in Romans 1, Paul begins Romans 2 addressing the real issue, the issue of "Sin." What is the "capital 'S'" offense in Romans 2:1–5?

The gospel announcement is that God's reign of kindness, not our sin, is the final word. As the woman somehow encountered that reign, experienced forgiveness, and responded in love, so we can

Bonus Activity:

Is it possible for someone to be "forgiven little"? What difference does our perception make, not on the forgiveness but on our appreciation of forgiveness? Discuss which is easier, to forgive or to be forgiven. By reading Romans 1–3 as a unit your group would have the opportunity to see the movement from our focus on human sin, however "big" or "little," to God's focus on "the redemption that is in Christ Jesus" (Romans 3:24).

SESSION TWO

Bonus Activity:
Ask for two volunteers. Have them face each other. One volunteer will change her or his expression, and the other will try to match it. Have them switch roles. Then have each look in a mirror and do the same. Which gave them a more accurate view of themselves?

Tip:
The harm done by disdain, resentment, and finger-pointing is the distancing from oneself and locating who I am not in myself but in my reactions to you.

Tip:
Take time for conversation about why it is that people feel the need to look down on someone else. Ask participants for hints on how to avoid doing that.

Tip:
Ask participants to observe a few seconds of silence. Ask one person to pray the prayer quietly while others close their eyes. Allow time for silence after the prayer.

be freed from our sin and our resentment and our dismissal of others to love.

Devotional Context

A very human reality in this text is the problem of resentment. The Pharisee shows us how we can resent and look down on either those who are worse than us (the woman in the city) or who we fear are better than us (Jesus, who wasn't the Pharisee's kind of prophet). Disdain, resentment, and finger-pointing not only break down human community, but they harm the one doing them.

1. Tell about a time in your life when you felt rejected or resented. How did that affect your feelings about yourself?

2. How can resenting or disdaining or willfully excluding someone make us weaker?

3. Discuss ways we can help each other be more accepting of others.

Wrap-up

1. If there are any questions to explore further, write them on chart paper or a whiteboard. Ask for volunteers to do further research to share with the group at the next session.

2. Ask participants for one new insight they have from this session—write them on the whiteboard or chart paper.

Pray

Dear Jesus, you bring God's rule of forgiveness and mercy and love into a world where rules are so often more important than people. Forgive us for turning our backs on others. Open us to the presence of your reign of kindness. Send us to love as you loved us. In your name we pray. Amen.

Extending the Conversation (5 minutes)

Homework

1. Read the next session's Bible text: Luke 8:26-39.

2. Make a list of people you "have trouble with"—either you are excluding them or they are excluding you. Pray for each of them by name each day this week.

3. Somehow the woman in the text heard a word of God's forgiveness before she met Jesus. List the people who have helped your faith life. If they are still living, write or talk to them to say thank you. If they are no longer living, thank God for them.

4. Write a list of at least four activities you can do that will share "great" love in response for "great" forgiveness.

Enrichment

1. Watch *A Pocketful of Miracles* (MGM, 1961). Discuss the stereotypes that influence how we see others. Where is great love shown? And . . . enjoy a very sweet movie!

2. Read "The Displaced Person," a short story by Flannery O'Conner. How does the story present the effects of judging some people less important than others?

3. Look at the ELCA website (www.elca.org) and find ways the ELCA seeks to reach out to those who have been excluded from church or society.

SESSION TWO

For Further Reading

Available from www.augsburgfortress.org/store:

Jesus and Judaism by E. P. Sanders (Minneapolis: Fortress Press, 1985). Sanders is the preeminent scholar of Judaism at the time of Jesus. His description of Pharisees is especially significant for understanding their relationship to Jesus and the early church.

Judaism in the Beginning of Christianity by Jacob Neusner (Minneapolis: Fortress Press, 1984). This Jewish scholar, who has been involved in Jewish/Christian conversations, presents a very readable summary of Judaism and the school of the Pharisees in the first century.

Looking Ahead

1. Read the next session's Bible text: Luke 8:26-39.

2. Read through the Leader Guide for the next session and mark portions you wish to highlight for the group.

3. Make a checklist of any materials you'll need to do the Bonus Activities.

4. Pray for members of your group during the week.

SESSION THREE

Luke 8:26-39

Leader Session Guide

Focus Statement
Jesus meets us to free us from fear and turn us to each other.

Key Verse
"Return to your home, and declare how much God has done for you." So he went away, proclaiming throughout the city how much Jesus had done for him.
Luke 8:39

Focus Image

When you're with me I fear . . . *less*. © Design Pics / SuperStock

Jesus Is Close to Those Estranged by Fear

Session Preparation

Before You Begin . . .

Almost everybody but Jesus is afraid in today's text. The **Gerasene** demoniac is a fearful figure. The demons in him are afraid of Jesus. The swineherds are frightened by what they see, the villagers are frightened by what they hear, and all the people of the area were scared by Jesus' power and asked him to go away. As a result of his encounter with Jesus, the demoniac is finally freed from fear and "in his right mind." This session can be a time to acknowledge what frightens us and ask for God's help. Give some thought to that yourself—what frightens you? How is God freeing you from fear?

Session Instructions

1. Read this Session Guide completely and highlight or underline any portions you wish to emphasize with the group. Note any Bonus Activities you wish to do.

2. If you plan to do any special activities, check to see what materials you'll need, if any.

3. Have extra Bibles on hand in case a member of the group forgets to bring one.

4. Read an article on demonic possession in a reputable biblical dictionary (such as *Interpreters Dictionary of the Bible* or *Anchor Bible Dictionary*).

5. Note that the opening and closing prayers involve use of a candle. Before lighting candles, check your local fire codes and your congregation's fire policies regarding the use of open flames.

Session Overview

The story of this text is about the victim of demonic possession who lives on the fringes of life. Jesus confronts the demons, orders them into swine, and frees the man. But the story is even more about bondage and freedom, fear and confidence, brokenness and community. Not only was the man bound by demons, but his neighbors were also "seized by fear." There is much that can be fearful in the world. Sometimes the fear we have can harm us as much as the things we fear. When fear threatens to paralyze

SESSION THREE

 Gerasene:
Most scholars place the setting of this story on the east shore of the Sea of Galilee near the modern settlement of El Kursi, which you can locate on a modern map of the area.

 Legion:
A division in the Roman army consisting of several thousand soldiers. In our time the term *battalion* might be used. It may be that the demon is saying this as a swipe at the Romans. And it may be that the demon does not want to share its name, since it was thought that to know another's name is to be able to have power against them.

us; rob us of trust in others, in ourselves, and in God; and tear communities apart, Jesus enters the scene to speak a word of freedom, trust, and community to us and through us.

HISTORICAL CONTEXT

Jesus and the disciples have crossed the Sea of Galilee to a town on the opposite shore. Scholars are not certain of the exact location, but it appears to have been a Gentile settlement on the east shore of the sea. It was not unusual for there to be communities of different ethnic groups living together in the Roman Empire. The Greek influence in the area was significant enough that many scholars assume Jesus spoke both Aramaic and Greek. If the settlement was Gentile, the unwritten conclusion is that the man with the **legion** of demons was also a Gentile.

The question of demonic possession continues to interest us, as movies and literature show. In the ancient world and pre-scientific age, illnesses involving bizarre behavior were especially attributed to demons and demonic possession. The Bible also contains many allusions to the disabling ability of fear to inflict madness and even death. We may have different views about what's behind such things, but the power of these conditions to shake and frighten us remains the same. There is a stability in being able to explain something that baffles. Jesus' appearance and authority evidenced by the healing of the man appear to have thrown off balance the Gerasenes' accepted explanation of why things are as they are—and that frightened them.

LITERARY CONTEXT

Jesus continues to reach out to the alien and the alienated. He literally and figuratively crosses chaos (immediately before this text is the stilling of the storm) with his disciples to encounter chaos controlling a Gentile. The setting heightens the sense of alienation—the man behaves like an animal; although alive, he lives with the dead; although in a family, he exists in terrible isolation.

This story also shows that Jesus, when confronted, does not defend himself. But when he finds the enemy confronting another, he acts always for the sake of the other. The texts in this session help participants to see Jesus' pattern of instruction. The fact that at the end of this confrontation Jesus is asked to leave the region, which he does, is not the final word. The final message is that the man "in his right mind" shares the good news.

Lutheran Context

In Luther's essay of 1539, "On the Councils and the Church," the reformer writes of the seven "Marks of the Church"—the indispensable elements that identify the Christian church. They are the possession of the Word of God, Holy Baptism, Holy Communion, the Office of the Keys (confession and forgiveness), the Office of the Ministry, worship, and the cross. By "the cross" Luther did not mean a symbol or decoration, but openness to suffering as part of discipleship.

Luther's **"theology of the cross"** confesses that God comes to us. We do not meet God in our false wishes, success, or when life is at its best, but rather God's incarnation meets us in those places where God chooses to be found—in our sin, our sickness, our weakness and distress. Jesus encounters the demoniac in the depths of despair and where there appears to be no hope.

Some forms of "reformed" theology, proceeding from Calvin, declare humans to be "totally depraved." Some forms of Christian theology known as **Arminian** look at human nature as somehow perfectible. Lutheran theology sees the human creature as created good but fallen. The Christian is "simultaneously justified and sinful." As such we can acknowledge the brokenness of the world without abandoning hope. The word as law points out such brokenness not only in demoniacs but in each of us. The word as gospel frees us from the finality of such brokenness and restores us to human life.

Devotional Context

Your group's devotional time can be a moment of revelation and insight—revelation and insight into realities in our own lives as well as revelation and insight into the way God chooses to free us from fear. The devotional context is the place where participants can ask the question that forms this chapter: "Where is God freeing us from fear?" and, more personally, "Where is God freeing *me* from fear?"

We meet much that is either fearsome or based on fear in today's text. We know that life in this world can be satisfying and frustrating, beautiful and ugly, freeing and binding, and delightful and fearsome. God's presence frees us from the need we often have to deny or ignore the more negative aspects of life. When we can acknowledge those areas of pain and fear, at least two things happen: we can ask God to come there to free us, and we can discover where God is already at work. Like the liberated

? Theology of the Cross:
This is a term coined by Luther in the Marburg disputation. Luther taught that we are to begin with what is revealed of God to learn of God and not to begin with theoretical or hypothetical knowledge of God. God's revelation is seen most amazingly on the cross of Christ. Theologians of the cross affirm that God is present and active not simply in those places where a theoretical god might appear, but in the struggles, pain, ambiguity, and sin of human life.

? Arminian:
Theological ideas named after a 16th-century Dutch theologian, Jacob Arminius, who taught that it was possible for Christians who applied themselves sufficiently to the task to live a life of perfect obedience to God.

SESSION THREE

demonic, hopefully we are then moved to share our stories of release from fear, rescue from bondage, and reintegration into grace-filled community.

Facilitator's Prayer

Gracious God, in Jesus you seek out and find all people. Please seek and find me, inspire me, help me to admit my own fears, and help me to rejoice in the freedom you give to live life with confidence. Amen.

Gather (10-15 minutes)

Check-in

Take time to greet each person and invite learners to introduce themselves to one another. Invite learners to share completed homework or any new thoughts or insights about the last session. Be ready to give a brief recap of that session if necessary.

Tip:
Invite those who have had time to read and think about today's text to say one thing they would like to learn from it.

Pray

Dear God of light and shadows, of certainty and uncertainty, of hope and fear, there is so much in this world that can frighten and make us want to run away. You, who travel with your people, be with us especially in those times to lead us from fear to wonder and from fleeing each other to living in faith and community. In Jesus' name. Amen.

Tip:
Begin the prayer in a softly lit room—light a candle. Read the prayer slowly and after each sentence of the prayer, pause to turn on more lights until the room is completely lit.

Focus Activity

Share moments in your life when you felt really afraid. Share also how you were able to move from that fear.

Look at the Focus Image and discuss:
- What do you think the women are reacting to?
- If you were one of them, what would you want to have happen?
- What is helping them to "fear . . . *less*"? What would you say if you wanted to comfort them?

Tip:
Before beginning, ask for definitions of *fear*. These could be phrases, sentences, or just one word. Write these down on the whiteboard or chart paper.

32 Close Encounters of the Jesus Kind Leader Guide

SESSION THREE

Open Scripture (10-15 minutes)

Ask for volunteers to read the parts of Jesus, the Gerasene, "Legion," the swineherds, and the local residents (you will need to rework the text with the parts of the swineherds and the residents as direct statements). Have the whole group give voice to the herd of swine.

Read the verses of Luke 8:22-25 in a responsive fashion to the session text as follows:

1. Luke 8:22, then Luke 8:26-27

2. Luke 8:23, then Luke 8:28-29

3. Luke 8:24, then Luke 8:30-33

4. Luke 8:25, then Luke 8:34-39

Read Luke 8:26-39.

Discuss how the story of the calming of the sea relates to and prepares us for what follows in the session text.

- Imagine a headline for this text as if it were a story in a newspaper.
- Who is afraid in this text and who is not afraid?
- How does Jesus transform "bondage" as seen in the comparison of verse 28 with verses 38-39?

Join the Conversation

Historical Context

This text continues the theme in Luke of Jesus going to those who are estranged and outcast. Hardly anyone could be more of a stranger than a man who had been familiar to the community and suddenly becomes a wild man—naked and uncontrollable and living, like a jackal, among the tombs.

1. Discuss how you might react upon encountering such a person. Who would you imagine to be the most fearful in this encounter?

Tip:
Write the answers for the first two questions on the whiteboard or chart paper. If there is time, compare the list of who is afraid and who isn't afraid with the definitions of *fear* supplied earlier.

Bonus Activity:
For more on the way Jesus and his followers faced their demons read Luke 4:33-41. How can the demons recognize Jesus, and why does he tell them to be silent about his identity? Check out Acts 19:13-16. What is the difference between this text and our text today? Like the session text, the text from Acts 19 has an element of humor to it. Take time to discuss the role of this humor.

Session 3: Luke 8:26-39   33

SESSION THREE

Tip:
Take time to discuss the kinds of conditions that can summon a response of fear. There are both physical and emotional/mental disorders that people find frightening or, at least very least, uncomfortable. Discuss these, the reasons for such reactions, and possible ways to counter these tendencies.

Bonus Activity:
If the church cemetery is next to the church or nearby, plan to go there and discuss what it would be like to encounter someone like the man in the text there. How does what we know about Jesus change the feeling of that place?

Tip:
Try to find an example of an elementary school lesson plan or a college syllabus to illustrate this discussion.

Bonus Activity:
Have copies available of Gerard Manley Hopkins (c. 1918) poem "Spring and Fall: To a young child." Read and discuss his line "It is Margaret you mourn for" in connection with reactions of fear. Websites like www.poets.org offer not only the text of the poem, but biographies of poets and supporting multimedia.

Bonus Activity:
Ask for examples from familiar books or literature that also have confrontations and resolutions (like Robin Hood and Little John). Especially ask for examples of persons who do not defend themselves but do defend others. You will want to have examples of your own to offer.

2. The power of fear to affect our well-being, sometimes to the point of madness, is well documented in the Bible. Read over the following passages and discuss the cause and effects of fear in each passage.
- Deuteronomy 28:28-34
- 1 Samuel 21:10-15
- Daniel 4
- Acts 5:1-11

In Jesus' day, such behavior was often attributed to demonic possessions. We might more readily speak of mental illness. Whatever the cause might be, wouldn't we agree with the Gerasenes that to encounter such a person could make us both fear him and fear what hidden power might lead him to such behavior?

3. How does Jesus address the situation in Luke 8:26-37? How did the fears of those on the scene change as a result? In what ways does what Jesus has to say in Luke 12:4-7 and Luke 24:36-43 help Christians to manage our fears today?

Literary Context

The broader context of this passage is the section of Luke presenting the teaching of Jesus in Galilee (Luke 3:1—9:50). His teaching is not like the valuable work of teachers in our time who are usually able to have a classroom, make lesson plans, and control the curriculum.

1. Jesus was teaching often as he traveled from one place to another in Galilee. His teaching was most often in the context of a challenge or confrontation. There are times when Jesus is threatened or challenged. Read Luke 4:23-30; Luke 5:33-39; Luke 6:1-5; and Luke 7:39-50. How does Jesus respond to attacks on himself?

2. More often Jesus exercises his power in situations that threaten someone other than himself. Read Luke 4:31-41; Luke 5:12-16; Luke 5:17-26; Luke 7:1-11; Luke 8:40-56; and Luke 9:37-43. What situations did Jesus encounter? How did he respond? In what ways is this a lesson for the church?

3. If the above passages were part of a course on discipleship, what do you think the teacher's objectives would be for the church today? Try to construct a syllabus from what you've experienced so far in this study: course title, catalog description,

objectives. Is it a 101 course or graduate level? What about Jesus' methods? Does he use multimedia, for example?

Lutheran Context

Lutheran theology has striven to be honest about God's promise of grace in Christ Jesus and also to be honest about the nature of the world—neither completely depraved, as some reformation traditions stated, nor perfectible, as some might wish. One of the "marks of the church" for Luther was suffering. That is, Christian people recognize the reality of the tragic in human life—situations such as we encounter in this text and such as those we encounter in our own lives. We cannot deny or ignore these situations.

1. Who is suffering in Luke 8:26-39? After compiling a list, read 1 Peter 4:12-15. Review your list through the lens of what Peter has to say about suffering. In what ways was this suffering to God's glory or not?

2. God's word as law helps us to know that things that are fearsome and binding are not simply out there but are also part of our makeup. What in our session text reveals the gospel—God's word of liberation to our captivity to fear and alienation?

The Lutheran concept of reading scripture for its "plain sense" permits us to not spend time debating whether the Gerasene is possessed by demons or mentally ill. Something tragic is taking place. Jesus reminds us in John 10:7-10 that the power that seeks to destroy life is around, seemingly not caring what life it destroys—a family man or a herd of swine. However, our theology of the cross proclaims that God is found precisely in those places we might not expect a nice God to be found—among the outcast, among the rejected, among the frightened and the frightening.

3. Come up with some examples of "wounded healers"—people whose experience of difficulty or suffering has made them better helpers for others. Discuss how the Gerasene man is such a person. How can our sufferings and struggles send us as healers as well?

Devotional Context

The story in our text is in many ways a story about fear. The fearsome Gerasene meets Jesus, but it is the demons that fear Jesus. The swineherds ran off in fear to the villages. When the people saw the man "in his right mind," they were afraid. Jesus frightened them, and they wanted him to leave.

Bonus Activity:

Share examples of how we tend to find sin and evil "out there." Is there any value in being able to recognize those things as part of our makeup?

Bonus Activity:

Read or sing Luther's hymn "A Mighty Fortress" (*ELW* 503, 504, or 505). How does this hymn illuminate our text today? Divide the verses between men and women with all joining on the last verse.

SESSION THREE

Tip:
First John 4:7-19 has some powerful things to say about the ability of God's love to "cast out fear." If time permits, meditation on this scripture could well enhance your conversation.

Bonus Activity:
Ask participants to write a prayer or a poem or draw an image that could help them turn their fears over to God.

Tip:
Ask the participants to make a list of what concerns or frightens them. They can do that during the week or, if there is time, at the session. Invite them to look at each of those words both as places to invite God and places where God is already working.

Tip:
Invite participants to pray the Lord's Prayer twice. The first time they should try to flex every muscle in their bodies—form a fist, grimace as hard as they can, and so on. The second time they should be restful and relaxed—either on the floor or on a soft chair. Discuss the difference it made in feeling bound or free.

Tip:
If you began the session with low light and a candle—light the candle again and, with each sentence in this prayer, turn off a light until only the candlelight remains. After the prayer, say, "The light shines in the darkness, and the darkness did not overcome it" (John 1:5).

We know that there is much about life in this world that is not only beautiful, joyful, and delightful, but also terrifying, destructive, and fearful. Try as they might, the people could not control the power that tormented the man. But they also could not control the fear that "seized them."

1. When have you felt powerless over something that seemed to control you? Have you been able to move beyond that control?

2. When have you felt so afraid that you also were "seized" like the Gerasenes (Luke 8:37)? In contrast, what did the love of Jesus liberate the demoniac to do (Luke 8:38-39)?

3. Stories about how we have been released or rescued from something fearful are powerful and helpful. Share with another person a way you were freed from fear or from what was fearful.

Wrap-up

1. If there are any questions to explore further, write them on chart paper or a whiteboard. Ask for volunteers to do further research to share with the group at the next session.

2. Ask volunteers to share a place or situation where they have experienced God freeing them from fear.

Pray

Loving Lord, you have walked with us throughout our lives. You know when we have been happy or sad, successful or unsuccessful, healthy or ill, assured or fearful, faithful or doubtful, hopeful or despairing. Whatever our condition, you have remained faithful to your decision to love us. Help us, dear God, when fear seizes us. Help us to know your presence that defeats all our enemies. Grant us patience in trial and give us voices to proclaim to all what you have done for us. In Jesus' name. Amen.

Extending the Conversation (5 minutes)

Homework

1. Read the next session's Bible text: Luke 9:51-62.

2. Make a list of what summons a fear response in you—these include people and situations, things that are inside of you and

things that are outside of you. In your daily prayers, offer these up to God for God's care and grace.

3. Reflect on the Focus Image for this study. Does anybody in the picture remind you of someone you know? If so, contact that person this week just to check in on him or her, strengthen your relationship, and share with each other how life has been.

Enrichment

1. Read from the end of this text to Luke 9:50. Note what conflicts and challenges appear and how Jesus addresses them. A new prediction of conflict arises in these verses. What is it?

2. Discuss with others what can bind and trap people in our world today—mental illness, hunger, and homelessness are a few examples. Can you take an active role in confronting any of these? With others in your group, develop a plan to be part of God's solution. Check out the ELCA website for ideas, for example www.elca.org/Growing-In-Faith/Ministry/Disability-Ministries/Mental-Illness.aspx.

3. Do an online search about "possession." Look for a variety of interpretations of what this might be.

For Further Reading

People of the Lie: The Hope for Healing Human Evil by M. Scott Peck (New York: Touchstone, 1998). Peck is a Christian psychiatrist who argues that "evil" ought to be a psychiatric category. He presents cases of people in various degrees of evil and argues that healing is available.

Available from augsburgfortress.org/store:

Many Forms of Madness: A Family's Struggle with Mental Illness and the Mental Health System by Rosemary Radford Ruether (Minneapolis: Fortress Press, 2010). Writing from her personal experience, the author relates the inhumane treatment throughout history of people with mental illness and calls on people to treat such sufferers with genuine care.

The Wounded Healer: Ministry in Contemporary Society by Henri Nouwen (New York: Doubleday, 1995). Nouwen writes about how the wounds we suffer can equip us to be more effective and compassionate healers.

SESSION THREE

The Real Satan: From Biblical Times to the Present by James Kallas (Minneapolis: Fortress Press, 1975). Kallas presents a balanced study of the ways in which Satan is manifest in such contemporary places and activities as drug and alcohol abuse, atheism, and in satanic worship, all the while giving assurance that Jesus Christ is victorious over all evil powers.

Looking Ahead

1. Read the next session's Bible text: Luke 9:51-62.

2. Read through the Leader Guide for the next session and mark portions you wish to highlight for the group.

3. Make a checklist of any materials you'll need to do the Bonus Activities.

4. Pray for members of your group during the week.

5. Visit a travel agency to ask for maps and materials on a trip from your area to Jerusalem to share in the next session.

SESSION FOUR

Luke 9:51-62

Leader Session Guide

Focus Statement

Jesus is in motion to change the world and invites us to move with him, sharing the hope of God's new day.

Key Verse

When the days drew near for him to be taken up, he set his face to go to Jerusalem. Luke 9:51

Focus Image

You want me to go where? © Design Pics / SuperStock

Jesus Is Close to Those Estranged by God's Distance

Session Preparation

Before You Begin . . .

The text for this day is the turning point of Luke's Gospel. Jesus "turns his face to go to Jerusalem," and the events are set in motion that will culminate in Jesus' death and resurrection. The one who had reached out to the alienated and alone now joins their ranks as one who "has nowhere to lay his head." As disciples, we are called to follow him on that journey.

Session Instructions

1. Read this Session Guide completely and highlight or underline any portions you wish to emphasize with the group. Note any Bonus Activities you wish to do.

2. If you plan to do any special activities, check to see what materials you'll need, if any.

3. Have extra Bibles on hand in case a member of the group forgets to bring one.

4. Bring in maps and brochures for a trip to Jerusalem from your location. Gather as many details and materials as possible. A topographical map from the time of Christ that shows the way from Galilee to Jerusalem and the location of Samaria would also be helpful.

5. Find and prepare to play in a recording of "You've Got to Walk that Lonesome Valley." If you have Internet access, you can find a very good version by Mississippi John Hurt on YouTube.

Session Overview

Jesus begins his travel to Jerusalem with a single-minded devotion to his task. He meets resistance, reluctance, and misunderstanding along the way. As disciples of Christ, we are called to accompany him. During this session, we will explore ways that we can be responsive to that call.

HISTORICAL CONTEXT

Jerusalem was literally and symbolically the center of religious and political power for the Jewish people as well as the ruling Romans. In Jesus' time, a movement toward Jerusalem could be

SESSION FOUR

> **? Travel narrative:**
> A particular kind of literature that gives the literal task of moving from one place to another the symbolic meaning of a significant change happening. The epic journey of the Lord of the Rings series does this. The narrative accounts of Abram/Abraham's journeys, the entry into Egypt and the exodus, Ruth's journey from her own people, and the exile and return of the people all use the geographic change to symbolize a spiritual change. Luke's narrative likewise uses geography to indicate the reality of change.

perceived by both as the final stage of a rebellion. James and John may have thought this to be the case since they responded to rejection by Samaritans with a desire for violent revenge. Jesus, however, is coming to Jerusalem not to gain power (as the powers of the world understand it) but to be betrayed and murdered for the sake of the world—God's ultimate outreach to the alienated.

Travel narratives in the Bible often mean something important is about to happen—Abram from Ur to Canaan (Genesis 14, 15), the movement of Israel into Egypt with Joseph (Genesis 46) and out of Egypt under Moses (Exodus 14 and following), the movement of Ruth from Moab to Israel (the book of Ruth), the exile to and return from Babylon—these all lead to a significant event. Jesus' turn to Jerusalem would be even more significant. To "set his face" (Luke 9:51) toward Jerusalem is Luke's way of saying that Jesus is now ready to make his move toward the cross.

Literary Context

Both Luke and Acts use geography as a literary device. It's a visual way to depict the expansion of God's kingdom though the proclamation of the gospel. Surprisingly, the introduction of John the Baptist in Luke 3:1-9 reverses expectations, urging us from the order of importance for *the world* to the order of importance for *the Word*. Bypassing Caesar and governors and high priests, the Word comes to John in the Wilderness. Beginning in these verses, the Word moves from the wilderness to Jerusalem and eventually onto Rome itself.

The three potential followers Jesus meets in this text are similar to those who were attracted to the early Christian community. Through very powerful and very personal figures of speech, Luke wants them to know that the call to follow Jesus is both challenging and urgent. The comforts of a home, religious duties, and family ties were all "blessings" that early Christians had to walk away from. The words of Jesus about his homelessness reflect the words of God to David when David wanted to build a home in Jerusalem (1 Chronicles 17:1-10). Luke's people and those to whom Jesus was speaking would recognize the similarity.

Lutheran Context

Lutheran theology is quick to identify discipleship as part of a living process. Luther's quote in today's session highlights daily life and vocation as that place where we learn how to follow Jesus. Jesus' call to complete obedience addresses us in our incompleteness as law—showing us our shortcomings and sin. But the fact that we, like Jesus in the text, are on the way and not yet there is gospel as well—we are on the way with Jesus, and the Holy Spirit is doing the work of "calling, gathering, enlightening, and sanctifying" God's people. Native American Lutherans have compared this balance of law and gospel to Plains Native ideas about movement along the **Red Road and Black Road**.

Lutheran theology is not a **"decision theology"** in the way American Evangelicalism defines it, yet it is very much involved in decisions. At each moment in our lives we are called to follow. Because we are on the way and not there yet, walking by faith, poor decisions cannot destroy us and good decisions cannot save us—only God's grace does that. This does not mean that Christians are incapable of Spirit-led decision making. Rather, this is what Jesus helps us with in Luke 9:51-62. Not only do we confront Jesus' own decision to make his move toward Jerusalem, but we are guided through some of the lesser decisions his followers would be faced with along the way.

Devotional Context

The idea of life as a journey can be a cliché, but it is one that is nevertheless true. We are involved in many journeys at any time in our lives the processes of family and school and work and relationships and travel and aging and on and on. As we hear of Jesus "walking that lonesome valley" we find a companion who knows something of our travel and our trials. We even find that God can appear to be an outsider as well, with no place to lay his head.

Our lives are so busy with our journeys that we don't often take time to think about them. The devotional exercise is designed to give participants a chance to think about the various roads they are on. As they consider them, they also are invited to remember that Jesus is on those roads with them. Encourage participants (and yourself) to take time regularly to look at these roads and consider ways we can be better followers of Jesus while we are on them.

Facilitator's Prayer

Dear Lord Jesus, you know what journeys I am on and you see all the paths that have led me to this time; you know the roads I will travel. Open me to your presence on all of them and help me to share to good news of that presence. Amen.

Red Road and Black Road:

From *Rivers of Life—Native Spirituality for Native Churches* by Paul Schultz and George Tinker (Minneapolis: Augsburg Fortress, 1988). Using Native concepts of ethics—spatial rather than temporal—the authors present the Plains Indian idea that, at any moment, we are at the crossroads of the Good Red Road of harmony and community and the Black Road of separation and manipulative power. Thinking temporally we might be afraid that we are so far gone on the Black Road that there's no chance at recovery— or so far along the Red Road that we can never go wrong. But since the intersection is always there, we are saved from despair or arrogance—just one step can turn us wrong or right.

Decision Theology:

A term used to describe the evangelistic tool of asking a person to make "a decision for Jesus" or pray the Jesus prayer, inviting him into one's heart. The popular view is that, once the decision is made, one becomes a Christian.

SESSION FOUR

Tip:
If you've found a recording of "You've Got to Walk that Lonesome Valley," you may decide to have it playing as participants come in.

Tip:
Make this a walking prayer. If you are in a building big enough, walk through hallways and rooms; begin the prayer after a few moments of travel and break it up to allow several minutes of journey and prayer. If you are not in a building large enough to do that and if weather permits, walk outside and pray the prayer in sections to allow several minutes of journey.

Tip:
Play or watch the recording of someone singing the folk song.

Gather (10-15 minutes)

Check-in

Take this time to connect or reconnect with the others in your group. Be ready to share new thoughts or insights about your last session. Share the homework activities that made a difference in your week. Invite someone who read the verses preceding today's session text to give a summary of them.

Pray

God, whose new day breaks upon us in the death, resurrection, and ascension of our Savior Jesus Christ, you have called us to share the good news of your love with our world. Fill us with the confidence your grace brings so that we might live and speak so that our world might also know, trust, and love you. In the name of Jesus. Amen.

Focus Activity

Look at the Focus Image for this session. Take turns describing what you see. What do you think precedes this photo and what will follow it?

An American folk song has these words: "You've got to walk that lonesome valley; You've got to walk it by yourself; Ain't nobody gonna walk it for you—You've got to walk it by yourself."

- How does this song and the photo relate to the Key Verse?
- How do they relate to your life?

Open Scripture (10-15 minutes)

Break up the text into parts—narrator, Jesus, James, John, and the three seekers. Encourage those speaking the parts to try each sentence with a different sound to their voice; that is, a harsh voice, a sympathetic voice, a challenging voice, a confused voice, or a defeated voice. Discuss how the tone of voice might change how we hear the text.

SESSION FOUR

Do an Internet search for photos of Jerusalem, a lightning strike, a fox in its den, a bird in its nest, a family gathered by a graveside, and a plow cutting a furrow. Project or display these photos as the portion of the session text that mentions those scenes is read. You might also want to close with a moment of meditation on a photo of the cross.

Read Luke 9:51-62.

- Who are the characters in this text? Who do you find yourself most drawn to or who do you identify with?
- Why does Jesus say, "The Son of Man has nowhere to lay his head" (Luke 9:58)?
- Do you think Jesus is being rude to the three who seem to want to follow him?

Join the Conversation (25-55 minutes)

Historical Context

Jerusalem—home to the house of God on Temple Mount and the site of the Roman governor—was the center of the Jewish people, and as important as playing in the Super Bowl to a contemporary football player. It was the place to go—for holidays, for reunions, for religious rites. It was the political, geographical, and spiritual center of the Jewish cosmos.

1. Who wouldn't want to go to Jerusalem? Read Psalm 122. What does this psalm tell you about the attitude of the Jewish people in regard to Jerusalem?

After Jesus' predictions of chapter 9 (Luke 9:21-23; Luke 9:31; Luke 9:44), the hearers of Luke's time should have come to recognize what the words "taken up" in Luke 9:51 would really mean.

2. Read the passages above and then discuss what is behind Luke's statement that Jesus "set his face" to go to Jerusalem. How does Luke 13:31-35 provide a humorous and hopeful side to what is otherwise very serious business for the Christ?

Bonus Activity:
Ask participants for a list of centers of power—political, religious, sporting, academic, and social. Write them on a whiteboard or chart paper as a way of helping to see how we view and how people of Jesus' time viewed power and importance. Look at the list of centers of power the group generated and ask which each member wants to visit and why.

Tip:
On a whiteboard or chart paper, draw a winding road that comes to a point in the distance. As group members read the verses, chart them on the road drawing. After the last verse is read, draw a cross at the end of the road.

Bonus Activity:
Share the materials you gathered for a trip to Jerusalem today. Discuss the difference between such travel and the simplicity and humbleness of Jesus' road.

SESSION FOUR

Tip:
The Jewish historian Josephus (born in 37 C.E.) speaks of the discord between Jews and Samaritans in his *Antiquities* (Book XX, ch. 6). You can find translations of this text online.

Bonus Activity:
In what ways does John 4 echo the teaching of Jesus in Luke 9:52-55? Have the group scan this passage for distinctions between Jews and Samaritans. Point them in particular to John 4:7-9 and 4:19-20. How does Jesus resolve these distinctions in John 4:13-14 and 21-24?

Bonus Activity:
Read the first chapter of the book of Jonah. Use a whiteboard or chart paper to compare the different responses to God's call in Jonah 1 and Luke 9.

Tip:
Chart these concentric circles on a whiteboard or chart paper and invite the group to think more symbolically than geographically. When thinking of our "Jerusalem" for example—who are those nearest to us, perhaps behind our walls and under our roofs, who need to see Jesus in our lives? Judea could be our neighborhood or town. Samaria might be thought of as those beyond the zone of comfortable relationships.

Tip:
Using the maps in their Bibles, have learners trace the movement in Luke 3 and the movement from Galilee to Jerusalem and beyond. Referencing a map of Paul's journeys would also be helpful for this activity. Check the Internet for maps that show the spread of Christianity beyond Bible times. For example: https://qed.princeton.edu/getfile.php?f=The_Origins_and_Spread_of_Christianity_to_AD_600.jpg.

3. The Samaritans and Judeans were Jews who disagreed on what was important and where it was important. But the time for religious violence and vengeance was past. Now was the time to move into God's new day.

- Read Luke 9:52-55. What were the Samaritans' attitudes about a prophet bypassing them and moving on to Jerusalem? How did the disciples take to their treatment?
- Read 2 Kings 1:9-16. Why does Jesus not make the Samaritan village suffer a similar fate? What does Jesus' rebuke of James and John teach us today?

Literary Context

Luke uses geography to proclaim the expanding of the good news of God's kingdom—the new day of God's rule. Luke 9:51 marks the beginning of the movement from Galilee to Jerusalem to Caesarea to Asia Minor and Greece and, finally, to the Empire's capitol in Rome. Jesus "sets his face" to go to Jerusalem, where he will be "taken up." The language indicates the utterly serious and intentional purpose of Jesus to accomplish what he has been sent to do.

1. Read Luke 3:1-9. What are the similarities and differences between this text and today's text, in which Jesus begins to move to Jerusalem and beyond?

2. How does the writer of Acts also use this geographical device in Acts 1:6-8? Brainstorm what could be today's equivalent of being witnesses in "Jerusalem, in all Judea and Samaria, and to the ends of the earth."

Jesus' use of figurative and metaphorical language when speaking to the three potential disciples in Luke 9:57-62 helps emphasize the dedication needed by those who follow God.

3. List the three figures of speech that Jesus employs in this passage. Discuss these figures of speech both in terms of what Jesus *is* saying and what he *is not* saying.
- Verses 57-58: _____
- Verses 59-60: _____
- Verses 61-62: _____

4. Read 1 Chronicles 17:1-10. How does this use of parallel passages help you understand what Jesus says in Luke 9:58?

Lutheran Context

Martin Luther wrote, "This life is not godliness, but growth in godliness; not health, but healing; not being, but becoming; not rest, but exercise. We are not now what we shall be, but we are on the way; the process is not yet finished, but it has begun; this is not the goal, but it is the road; at present all does not gleam and glitter, but everything is being purified" ("A Defense and Explanation of All Articles," *Luther's Works* 32:24).

1. In what ways does this quote describe what is happening in the session text?

Only Christ can be completely obedient—he walks this road and calls us to follow. This call speaks to us as law as we see our own shortcomings and reluctance to follow. In some Christian circles, the believer is called to "make a decision for Christ" and thus become Christian. Without denigrating the value of that call, Lutherans look to God's decision to call us. This doesn't free us from deciding. Rather, it reminds us that all of life is lived in response to Christ's call to follow and proclaim. Our failure in one instance or our success in another does not determine God's love but can open us to God's gracious will.

2. According to Luke 9:57-62, following Jesus seems like a very difficult path. How does God's love in the following passages help us to put that path into perspective?
- Matthew 11:25-30
- 2 Corinthians 4:5-10
- Hebrews 12:1-4

Tip:
For example: Jesus' own emotion-filled attendance at Lazarus's graveside in John 11 proves that the Lord himself was touched by the pangs of grief in the face of death. Jesus *is not* asking his followers to be heartless, but he *is* asking us to be even more concerned about sharing the Word of life that enables us and others to manage losses with faith, hope, and love.

Bonus Activity:
Listen to the song "Is That All There Is?" famously recorded by Peggy Lee, and discuss the difference it makes to see ourselves as a work in process rather than being all we will be.

Tip:
Remind participants that it isn't our faith or the quality of our faith that saves us, but God's grace is always in the process of creating faith in us.

Bonus Activity:
Share the Native American understanding of our life journey from the Session Overview. Then create a "Red Road/Black Road" experience by having two volunteers be blindfolded. Each will be asked to go to another room and bring back a glass of water. Turn each around a few times. The first will have no instructions and will probably not be able to continue, the second will be carefully instructed which way to turn by the group. Discuss how each felt about the exercise. Compare the exercise to a life or spirituality in which there are few second chances. And then compare the experience to a life or spirituality in which at any moment we can return to balance.

SESSION FOUR

Devotional Context

Jesus is beginning the final journey of his earthly ministry. He is traveling down a road that he knows will end at the cross, yet he moves with faith and determination. We also travel down many paths and many roads, not just in our life in the long haul, but each day.

1. Take time for silence, closing your eyes while one of your group members reads the session text again. Remain in silence for a while and imagine the scene described—the people involved, the terrain, the sounds of the earth around and underfoot. Imagine yourself in the scene as well. Where are you? What are you doing and feeling? After some silence, share what you experienced.

2. Write down a list of the "roads" you are currently on. Then rewrite the list beginning with the words, "I am with Jesus on the road to . . ."

Tip:
Play "You've Got to Walk that Lonesome Valley" again as people write their responses.

Wrap-up

1. If there are any questions to explore further, write them on chart paper or a whiteboard. Ask for volunteers to do further research to share with the group at the next session.

Bonus Activity:
Discuss how some of our "roads" have helped us walk with others on their roads. Why is that the case? Who has helped us on our walks?

2. The three seekers in the text had "obstacles" that might have made following Jesus difficult—the comfort of a home, the inability to cope with loss, and the need to be in touch with family. What obstacles do we have?

Pray

Dear Lord Jesus, we don't often respond as well as we should or could to your call to follow. We don't always make the right decisions regarding which paths to take. Yet, amazingly, you continue to call us, you continue to trust us to proclaim the kingdom, and you continue to walk with us. Forgive us our failures and give us your Spirit to grow into faith. Be with us on our roads and, at the end, gather us to yourself. Amen.

Tip:
Have participants sit or stand in different parts of the room and divide the prayer among the various participants—we are in different places on our journey, but we journey with the same God and the same prayer.

Extending the Conversation (5 minutes)

Homework

1. Read the next session's Bible text: Luke 10:1-11, 16-20.

2. Draw a "life map" of your faith journeys and to share significant elements of that map with each other. Write a "Prayer for People on the Way" for all who are on life's journey.

3. Do you know somebody who is walking a difficult path just now—illness, economic difficulties, a student facing homework, a soldier oversees, or maybe someone just a bit worn out? Contact that person to let him or her know you're thinking of and holding him or her in prayer.

4. Jesus invites one of the questioners to "proclaim the kingdom of God." Develop a list of four ways you can share the kingdom with others—both actions and words. Be especially mindful of the "Samaritans" in your life. Look for opportunities to try each of these ways and be ready to share with the members of your group.

Enrichment

1. Using libraries or Internet searches, find a work of art that illustrates what a journey of faith might be.

2. Look through *Evangelical Lutheran Worship* for hymns you find appropriate to help the faithful in their Christian journey. Make one of those hymns part of your devotions during the week ahead.

3. Jesus speaks of the Son of Man not having a place to lay his head. Homelessness remains a problem. Do some research to find homeless shelters close to you. Contact them to find out ways you can help.

4. Using either the ELCA Yearbook or the ELCA website, find where global missions are proclaiming the kingdom of God. Learn about ways that you can partner in this proclamation.

SESSION FOUR

For Further Reading

Available from augsburgfortress.org/store:

Imaging the Journey: . . . of Contemplation, Meditation, Reflection, and Adventure by Mark C. Mattes and Ronald R. Darge (Minneapolis: Kirk House Publishers, 2007). This book is an invitation to meditate on the journey of faith using images from art as well as devotional meditation.

Bound and Free: A Theologian's Journey by Douglas John Hall (Minneapolis: Fortress Press, 2005). Canadian theologian Douglas John Hall reviews his life journey of responding to the call of Christ to follow.

Looking Ahead

1. Read the next session's Bible text: Luke 10:1-11, 16-20.

2. Read through the Leader Guide for the next session and mark portions you wish to highlight for the group.

3. Make a checklist of any materials you'll need to do the Bonus Activities.

4. Pray for members of your group during the week.

5. Read verses 12-15 in the text. Why do you think they have been left out of the session text? Do you agree with that?

SESSION FIVE

Luke 10:1-11, 16-20

Leader Session Guide

Focus Statement

Jesus is not alone in his mission but invites all who are called to join him in calling others with the good news of the nearness of God's kingdom.

Key Verse

Whatever house you enter, first say, "Peace to this house!" Luke 10:5

Focus Image

Come to the table! © SuperStock RF / SuperStock

Jesus Is Close to Those Seeking the Estranged

Session Preparation

Before You Begin ...

In this session, we will read about Jesus commissioning coworkers to help him seek out and call others into God's new day. In the course of the study, learners will consider the invitations they have received and given. They will explore ways to continue inviting brothers and sisters into God's community of grace.

Session Instructions

1. Read this Session Guide completely and highlight or underline any portions you wish to emphasize with the group. Note any Bonus Activities you wish to do.

2. If you plan to do any special activities, check to see what materials you'll need, if any.

3. Have extra Bibles on hand in case a member of the group forgets to bring one.

4. Have one large candle and enough small candles for each person in the group. Before lighting candles, check your local fire codes and your congregation's fire polices regarding the use of open flames.

Session Overview

How is God inviting strangers into the community of grace? This session focuses on how Christ uses people to call other people into the community of faith. We will hear of the instructions to "the seventy" and discuss how the faithful continue to be sent out to call in.

HISTORICAL CONTEXT

In first-century Palestine, neither itinerant teachers nor beggars were rare occurrences. Jesus' words about not greeting people on the road were meant to show that his **apostles** were not simply wandering teachers but on a specific mission. His instructions that they remain in one house in each place would also differentiate them from the beggars who were common at the time as well. These sent ones were not sent as beggars but as workers who deserved their pay (Luke 10:7b). Participants should be encouraged to share times when they were "sent" on a specific

SESSION FIVE

Apostolic:
From the Greek verb *apostello* (apo-STEL-lo), which means "to send out." An apostle is one who has been sent out on a specific mission by one in authority. The term was used in diplomatic circles in the ancient world. New Testament authors borrowed it to speak of those who have been "sent out" by God.

and important task. The church is **apostolic** not in its pedigree—where it comes from—but in its pedestrian mission—where and to whom it is going.

Who are we inviting to gather around the inclusive table of God's grace? As was true for the seventy in ancient Palestine, table fellowship in the church indicates more than a casual relationship between those at the table. Jesus reminds those sent that they are going to be part of the community. We are not fly-by-night, fast food purveyors of the "bread of life." The church is called to be fully present, as Jesus is fully present in the sacrament of his supper. We love and serve, inviting the estranged to be family.

Literary Context

There are several literary devices and allusions Luke uses in this text both to tie the action to the history of Israel and to point, as Luke does, to the wider theme of the geographic extension of the proclamation of the gospel. While the multiplication of Jesus' ministry among his followers in Luke 10 continues to inform and inspire the church's mission today, we recognize that resistance to the gospel both from without and from within is to be expected.

Numerology:
The study of numerical patterns in the Bible and their literary significance. The numbers 3, 4, 7, 10, 12, 40, and 1000 (along with variations of their sums and products) are used repeatedly in Scripture to convey ideas of perfection, creation, completeness, emphasis, community, trial, and vastness.

An understanding of how the Bible uses numbers in symbolic ways is called **numerology.** The use of the number 70 has several Old Testament parallels. First, Jesus sends out 70 "apostles." The early reader would recall both Moses' selection of 70 helpers (Numbers 11:10-30). Jesus' sending of the 70 does not mean that only 70 can be witnesses to God's new day. But it means that there are those who "share in peace" (Luke 10:6a) who are already out there. In addition, 70 is the number of nations of the world according to Genesis 10. Early hearers would understand the 70's mission as symbolic—going to all the nations. Luke consistently points to the extension of God's grace to all.

Dualistic:
Any worldview that pictures the world as made up of two equal and competing realities—one good and the other evil. Ancient Israel encountered dualistic religions in Persia. Dualistic religions such as Mithraism and Zoroastrianism were part of the Mediterranean world at the time of Jesus. There were also early Christian heresies that were dualistic.

The character of Satan is one familiar to Luke's hearers. Other ancient religions looked at the world in a **dualistic** way—roughly equal division between the forces of good and the forces of evil. Judaism did not think this way. Satan is never God's equal, but the voice that brings accusations against God's people and against God. If heeded this voice has the power to paralyze the proclamation of the gospel. But the promise in passages like Romans 8:31-39 is that God's grace speaks a better word—the empowering word of love.

Lutheran Context

The Lutheran Context outlines two significant Lutheran contributions to the identity of the believer. When Jesus speaks of the seventy as "lambs [in] the midst of wolves" (Luke 10:3a), we may be tempted to think of those inside the church as "lambs" and those outside as "wolves." But Luther reminded us that Christians are both justified and sinful. By this Luther meant that God in Christ forgives our sins, yet our sinful nature, our sinful tendencies—our sin—remains. We are on the way and not there yet. In the midst of our sin, however, we live as forgiven and justified persons. We can be freed either from self-glorification or self-loathing in the honest recognition that we are both lamb and wolf.

Luther also freed the world from the medieval concept of **vocation**. During Luther's time, the common view was that only clergy had a calling from God. Luther's reading of Scripture said "No!" to such a view. All useful work is a calling from God. In that work, we serve our neighbors and glorify God. In the context of our daily lives, we serve God not only by "making good shoes" but also by telling others about Jesus from the perspective of our own graced imperfection. These freedoms are what enable us all, both cobbler and cleric, to labor for God's harvest with both confidence and joy.

Vocation:
From the Latin word *vocatio*, meaning a calling that comes from one person to another. In Christian theology, God is the one who calls (light out of darkness, life out of death), and God calls each person into faith and into the place in life from which he or she can serve neighbor and world.

Devotional Context

Learners are asked to look at ways they have been told the love of Jesus by others and how they can do the same. God's call to us in baptism is also God's call to us to share the good news with all people—especially the "estranged," those who have been seen to be outside the arena of God's activities.

The church is **evangelical**. This does not mean that our primary business is go make others think as we do; rather, it means that we are grounded in the gospel of God's decision to justify the ungodly. As we grow in appreciation of that, we also wish to share that good news with others—that God's love and presence is not just for *me* but for *you*. Urge participants to encourage one another to remember how the gospel was brought into their lives, give thanks for those who did so, and share ways each can share God's good news in his or her own particular way.

Evangelical:
A word that comes from the Greek word for "good news," or rather the announcement of the good news. In much of American Christianity, the term has to do with the task of converting others. In Lutheran language, it means to be grounded in the gospel—the primary activity is God's. As we realize and rejoice in that, we move to our activity of serving and proclaiming.

Facilitator's Prayer

Dear God, I thank you that you ask someone like me to lead other people like me! Give me grace in that calling to ground myself in the good news of your love so that I might share with others in that grace. In Jesus' name. Amen.

SESSION FIVE

Gather (10-15 minutes)

Check-in

Take this time to connect or reconnect with the others in your group. Be ready to share new thoughts or insights about your last session. Share with each other any material from last week's homework assignments.

Pray

God of grace, you have always delighted to draw near to your creation, calling the estranged into your community of grace and empowering them to speak your invitation in your name. Thank you for loving us enough to trust us with your word of grace. Help us seek ways to seek others that all might rejoice in your new day of peace. We ask this in Jesus' name. Amen.

Focus Activity

Tip: Alert learners before you begin what the activity encompasses and what they need to do and say. In the discussion that follows, help them to describe the effect of the increased light as each candle was lit. Talk about the difference between the brightness of electric lights and the lights of candles that allow the reality of shadows and darkness to be a part of our experience. The text and the study for today speak of the reality of both light and darkness—lambs and wolves, insiders and outsiders of the Christian life.

Note: for this activity arrange chairs in a circle. Each person should be given a small candle and briefed on their responses. After lights are turned off, set a large candle in the middle, proclaiming, "The light of Christ!" All respond, "Thanks be to God." One person will be invited to light his or her candle from the large candle and take the light to another member's candle. That person does the same to another until all candles are burning. Take time to look around at each other in the candlelight. End by saying, "We are all in God's image." All respond, "Thanks be to God."

Take time to talk about the exercise. What did you see from the time the lights were off to the time all the candles were burning? Note the different sights people describe. Remember the exercise as we read about Jesus sending 70 people to invite "outsiders" into the light of God's kingdom.

Open Scripture (10-15 minutes)

Have the group form pairs to read the text. Ask each pair to summarize the text in one sentence and then make a drawing to illustrate that summary. When all have finished, read the text together and share the drawings and explanations for them.

> OR

As one person reads the text—slowly enough to allow careful listening—ask participants to listen to words of promise and words of direction/orders. Ask them to raise their right hands when they hear words of promise and left hands when they hear directions or orders.

Read Luke 10:1-11, 16-20.

- How do you think the 70 felt when they were first sent out on their mission? Do you think their feelings changed in the course of their mission?
- What does it mean that Satan fell from heaven like a lightning flash?
- What do you think it means to have one's name "written in heaven" and why would that be better than having the authority the 70 possessed?

Join the Conversation (25-55 minutes)

Historical Context

Religious itinerants were not unusual in the time of Jesus, and neither were beggars who counted on the good will of those who wished to do something good for someone else. Jesus draws a sharp distinction between such persons and the "seventy others" of Luke 10:1-2. The 70 functioned as emissaries, "apostles"—those who are sent out. *Apostolic* doesn't mean so much who touches whose head as it means where obedient feet go in Jesus' name.

1. How does Jesus describe the "professional ethics" of those sent out in his name in Luke 10:1-11? How does the church remain "apostolic" today?

You have already been invited to dine with Jesus in Luke 7:36-50. This was one of many moments that Jesus and his disciples shared the bread of life (John 6:35-40) while breaking the bread of fellowship (Acts 2:42-47). Table fellowship remains a significant sign of community in the Middle East. The meals shared by the 70 confirmed the welcome of the good news.

 Tip:
We don't have too many itinerant preachers or beggars going from door to door, but we do have telemarketers! Ask participants to discuss ways a Christian sharing God's good news with others should be different from telemarketing. No set script, no cold calls, not trying to sell something, but seeking to give something—these are among the differences.

 Tip:
Apostolic succession is the belief in some denominations of Christianity that there is an unbroken line of spiritual authority passed through the laying on of hands in ordination from the first apostles to present-day clergy. For more on this go to: www2.elca.org/lutheranpartners/archives/histepi.html.

 Bonus Activity:
Bring copies of two recent issues of *The Lutheran* magazine. Ask learners to spend five minutes looking through the magazines to find examples of how the ELCA is being "apostolic" in the way described in this section.

SESSION FIVE

Tip:
For the sake of time, divide the group around each of these "meals." Instruct them to get a general feel for the situation and to settle on a word that describes it. They should prepare to summarize the passage and explain why they chose the word they did.

Bonus Activity:
Have learners look at the Focus Image for this session. What is the mood around the table? What kinds of things may have led to such a gathering? Then ask participants to think of giving a dinner party. Ask them to write down the kinds of people they would like to be there and the kinds they would not want to be there. Discuss the results in the context of Jesus' words to the disciples.

Bonus Activity:
Bring in a map of your area—the community, county, state, and region. Ask participants to suppose they were the earliest church and then propose a geographic strategy for the spread of the good news using this map. Discuss what made them choose this strategy. Why do they think the early church expanded as it did?

Tip:
Satan is a Hebrew word that means "accuser" or "prosecuting attorney." "The Satan" is never God's equal—always more of a trickster or a bringer of chaos. Some in the group may be unfamiliar with the presentation of Satan in the book of Job. Try not to get sidetracked by stories of the "fall of Lucifer" or discussion of how Satan came about, but look at Satan's role as accuser, tempter, and troublemaker in Jewish thought.

2. Scan the following occasions of table fellowship in Luke. Discuss what is the same and what is different about these meals. What kind of estrangement is being addressed in these meals? Try to agree on one word that summarizes the purpose of each.
- Luke 14:1-24 is a meal of: _____
- Luke 19:1-10 is a meal of: _____
- Luke 22:7-23 is a meal of: _____
- Luke 24:13-53 is a meal of: _____

Literary Context

The numerology of both the sum and product of the numbers 7 and 10 in the Bible can offer some fascinating insights—7 being a number of wholeness and 10 being a number that intensifies the power and perfection of any associated number.

1. Look up Genesis 10. The 70 descendents of Noah listed here summarize this early census of the world's population. How might this fit with Luke's geographic theme as it relates to the progress of the gospel?

2. Read Numbers 11:10-30. What was the purpose of these 70? Is Moses being restrictive or expansive in how the gift of prophesy is exercised here? How does Numbers 11:29 relate to the session text?

The 70 are given authority over all that challenges God's will for the good, as represented by Satan, snakes, and scorpions (Luke 10:17-20). This authority is not for the sake of showing power but joyously proclaiming the presence of heaven—God's gracious rule with God's people.

3. Read Job 1:6-12 and Job 2:1-8. What is the picture of Satan presented here? What is the image of the "heavenly court"? How does Romans 8:1, 31-39 state the reason for our joy despite the accusations and influences of evil today?

Lutheran Context

Jesus speaks of the 70 as "lambs [in] the midst of wolves." Lutheran theology understands that there is always resistance to the word. This resistance is never simply "out there," but it is always a part of each believer.

1. In what ways does the session text speak to this resistance? How does Luther's description of Christians—that we are at the same time justified and sinful—speak to dilemmas within ourselves when it comes to being sent out as "laborers into his harvest"?

2. Read Revelation 21:22-27. This is a text of promise written to people who were being persecuted for their faith. In what ways does this text expand our understanding of the sending of the 70 and the mission of the church today?

The word of grace doesn't proceed from either believers or the church because of our perfection but rather because of God's grace. Jesus tells the 70 not to rejoice over their deeds of power, as significant as these were, but because their "names are written in heaven." Our joy doesn't come from how important, strong, or significant we might be, but it comes from the reality of God's choice to be present in our lives. Neither is our significance diminished if we are not "important" or strong or rich. The "drawing near of the kingdom of God" in Christ makes us one with Christ and the saints of all time.

3. Luther revolutionized the way Christian people looked at themselves when he spoke of vocation—our "calling" consisting not in being clergy or monks but in doing our faithful duties and thus witnessing to God. The reformer is widely attributed to have said, "A Christian cobbler makes good shoes, not inferior shoes with crosses on them." How does this saying relate to Luke 10:3? In what ways does 1 Corinthians 1:18-31 provide you the confidence to "go on your way"?

 Bonus Activity:
Ask the participants to think of difficult assignments they have had in their lives—how they felt when they received the assignment and how they felt when they were finished with it (and whether it went well or not so well).

 Tip:
Much of popular Christianity in America is not comfortable with Luther's paradox that the Christian is at the same time justified and a sinner. Participants may also be uncomfortable with such thinking. Help them to understand the honest humanity of such a position and how that can save us from too much arrogance ("I'm perfect!"—"Well, no you're not—check things out—sin is still around!") or too much self-hatred ("I'm so imperfect and sinful!" "Well, that could be, but, as Luther's friend Johan Staupitz put it, 'Don't be so bold as to think you can out-sin the grace of God'").

 Bonus Activity:
What if the NFL commissioner rules that only the 22 starters for the winning team of the Super Bowl will receive Super Bowl rings and the prize money. Discuss whether this is fair or not. How does that relate to Jesus' advice that what brings joy is not their accomplishments but that their names are "written in heaven."

 Bonus Activity:
Ask each participant to think about this line and then supply a phrase to finish it: "I may be a sinner, but because of God's grace I . . ." Write down the answers on the whiteboard or chart paper.

SESSION FIVE

Tip:
Take time for silence. Ask participants to write the names of those who shared the good news with them over the course of their lives.

Bonus Activity:
Have copies of *Evangelical Lutheran Worship* available and invite musicians to lead the group in singing "There Is a Balm in Gilead" (*ELW* 614)

Devotional Context

The spiritual "There Is a Balm in Gilead" has these words: "If you cannot preach like Peter, if you cannot pray like Paul, you can tell the love of Jesus and say he died for all" (*ELW* 614). You are participating in this study because at some points in your life someone told you about Jesus. Think about parents, Sunday school teachers, friends, strangers, or others who have in some way opened you to Jesus.

1. Imagine a dinner table at which all who have had an impact on your faith life are sitting and enjoying a happy meal. Who is there? What is the conversation about? Is there anyone not there who should be?

We all have been called to share the good news of the nearness of God's kingdom. We don't all do that alike, but we all do that with the gifts we have. It is good to remember with thanksgiving those who have led us to faith and to remember with hope those with whom we share God's good news.

2. Read Acts 8:25-38. What opportunities have you had to speak a word of grace and invitation to others? How do you feel about their response?

3. Looking at the Focus Image again, make lists of how such a gathering is like Holy Communion and how it is not. In what ways can your church's celebration of the Lord's Supper be more like the "heavenly banquet" of Luke 14:7-14?

Wrap-up

1. If there are any questions to explore further, write them on chart paper or a whiteboard. Ask for volunteers to do further research to share with the group at the next session.

2. Ask participants to share how their particular "vocation" provides them with opportunities to share God's good news.

3. As this is the next to last session in this Book of Faith unit, discuss what's next for your group. Discuss how group members could serve to multiply the Book of Faith ministry through invitation of others and the initiation of new Bible studies.

Pray

Dear God, your reign and its new day of grace is always near. We thank you for all you have called to be a part of the community of the church. We thank you for making us a part of that community. Open us to your invitation to go and prepare others to receive your new day. Give us love and grace and hope in our daily tasks. In Jesus' name. Amen.

 Tip:
If you did the exercise in Lutheran Context in which you finished the phrase, "I may be a sinner, but because of God's grace . . ." then begin the prayer by praying, "We thank you, God, that we can . . ." and then read the responses before moving into the closing prayer.

Extending the Conversation (5 minutes)

Homework

1. Read the next session's Bible text: Luke 10:25-37.

2. Prepare a meal (or host a potluck) for people in your group; invite them to your house and enjoy table fellowship.

3. Make a list of people who have helped shape your faith life. For those who are alive, find them and send them a thank-you note. Pray a prayer of thanksgiving for those no longer alive.

4. Tell one person about Jesus this week. Share with others in your group how that felt for you.

Enrichment

1. Watch the movie *Babette's Feast* (Word Films, 1988). This is a moving story of the power of love and fellowship to invigorate faith and restore human community.

2. Staying with the foreign movie theme, watch *Jésus of Montréal* (Orion Classics, 1990) for a representation of how "telling the story" can bring Jesus into the life of the teller.

3. Dig into biblical numerology. One interesting online overview can be found at www.biblestudy.org/bibleref/meaning-of-numbers-in-bible/1.html. Just beware—while it's fascinating stuff, some people take numerology too far.

4. Read the Acts of the Apostles, underlining each instance of someone sharing the news of the kingdom.

SESSION FIVE

> **For Further Reading**
>
> Available from augsburgfortress.org/store:
>
> *The Evangelizing Church: A Lutheran Contribution*, ed. Richard H. Bliese and Craig Van Gelder (Minneapolis: Augsburg Fortress, 2005). This is both a historical review of Lutheran evangelism and a guide to congregations seeking to evangelize in the 21st-century world.
>
> *Listen! God Is Calling! Luther Speaks of Vocation, Faith, and Work* by D. Michael Bennethum (Minneapolis: Augsburg Fortress, 2003). This book centers around Luther's advice on vocation and its application to the church today.

Looking Ahead

1. Read the next session's Bible text: Luke 10:25-37.

2. Read through the Leader Guide for the next session and mark portions you wish to highlight for the group.

3. Make a checklist of any materials you'll need to do the Bonus Activities.

4. Pray for members of your group during the week.

5. Look for examples of "good Samaritans" in the week ahead—look in newspapers, television news, shows, movies, and your daily life.

SESSION SIX

Luke 10:25-37

Leader Session Guide

Focus Statement

The God who seeks and saves the lost uses our own life experiences—even those of loss and alienation—to help us become more effective and loving helpers.

Key Verse

Jesus said . . . , "Go and do likewise." Luke 10:37b

Focus Image

Surprising service from unexpected sources.

Jesus Is Close to Those Learning from the Estranged

Session Preparation

Before You Begin . . .

This last session of the series is a good time to take stock of how you feel about the process so far. Think about and pray for each member of the group. To prepare for this session, think about times in your life when you have received unexpected help, and times when you may have given such help.

Session Instructions

1. Read this Session Guide completely and highlight or underline any portions you wish to emphasize with the group. Note any Bonus Activities you wish to do.

2. If you plan to do any special activities, check to see what materials you'll need, if any.

3. Have extra Bibles on hand in case a member of the group forgets to bring one.

4. Read the text for today several times, trying consciously to "live the text" from the perspectives of each of the characters (Jesus, the lawyer, the wounded traveler, the Levite, the priest, the Samaritan, and the inn keeper).

Session Overview

This session will help us to focus on the good news of God's finding and healing us as the basis of our call to care for others—not because it will get us to heaven, but simply because others need our help.

HISTORICAL CONTEXT

The lawyer in this text is often presented as an opponent of Jesus or simply a difficult person. Down to our own time, a significant aspect of **rabbinical** learning is that one shows respect to another by arguing—and trusting that truth will emerge in the course of the argument. This view assumes that nobody has a market on the truth but that by argument, debate, question and answer, and collaboration, the truth will emerge. One way to demonstrate this is to have each person in the study group have a few pieces from a set of building blocks. As each adds his or her piece in properly, a building emerges.

SESSION SIX

> **Rabbis:**
> Teachers who were steeped in the scriptures and the sacred writings and traditions of Judaism. While Israel was still a nation and the temple stood, the rabbis helped interpret the faith that was made secure in the temple for the ordinary lives of people. After the destruction of Israel and the dispersion of Jewish people throughout the world, rabbinical Judaism became the norm and rabbis continued to teach, debate, and interpret Judaism to make it alive in the daily lives of believers.

> **Samaritans:**
> A people who were (and still are) descendants of Jews who were not exiled to Babylon in the sixth century B.C.E. The name comes from the Hebrew word *shamar*, which means to "keep or observe" the Torah. While the Jews were in exile for six decades, the Samaritan community developed separate rituals and traditions, observed sacrifice at its own site (not Jerusalem), and were regarded by the rest of the Jewish community as heretical. There still is a small Samaritan community in modern Israel.

> **Good works:**
> These are often seen as "bad works" by Lutherans. An early Lutheran theologian, Nicholas of Amsdorf, claimed they were actually harmful for salvation. The phrase is often used as shorthand for "doing good works in order to get to heaven." Such good works are neither ethical nor theologically proper. It's as though we're just using our neighbor to get to heaven. Passages like John 15 and Galatians 5, however, describe genuinely good works as "fruits of the Spirit." They are qualities of godly living that organically and spontaneously stem from our faith in Jesus.

The road between Jerusalem and Jericho was a dangerous place—a place where robbers could easily hide. All of us know of such places in our own areas—bad parts of town or dangerous, lonely roads. In addition to the prevalence of bandits, there was always the chance one might run into another kind of undesirable. The **Samaritans** were considered bad enough. They were Jewish relatives who weren't accepted into the family of Judaism—untrustworthy, lower class, and deceitful. Again, human beings are good at emphasizing such differences. The group can talk about current "in crowds" and "out crowds" in their communal or personal experience.

Literary Context

The text follows Jesus' words in Luke 10:21-24 highlighting the accessibility of God's new day not for the wise and important but for the "infants" and those who are hearing "right now". The form of the text is the presentation of a problem, the presentation of a means to a solution, and the solution. Mathematicians and engineers would understand the process!

The vocabulary of Luke provides a startling confession. We return again to the word translated as "moved with pity" (Luke 10:33), the marvelously difficult-to-say Greek verb *splagchnizomai* (*splangk-NIZ-o-mai*), which comes from the word *splangchnon*, which means "guts"! This is a visceral feeling of intense love and mercy and pity. The startling thing about this word is that it was also used in Luke 7:13 (Jesus seeing the widow at Nain in our first session) and Luke 15:20 (the father of the prodigal son). This is a word descriptive of God's reaction to lost humans. The Samaritan—an outsider—both represents God and those who have been touched by God's mercy for them.

Lutheran Context

Two aspects of a Lutheran understanding of ethics and Christian living are discussed in this session. First of all, Lutherans are not against **good works**! We are against good works that are only good for us. Justifying oneself, as we see in Luke 10:29, runs counter to the doctrine of justification by grace through faith that Luther saw in Galatians, Romans, and elsewhere in the New Testament. This grace, which we have freely received from God in Christ, compels us to love likewise. Good works do not belong to us, Luther said, but to our neighbor. God's love and forgiveness frees us from wearing ourselves out to get to heaven. Our work is freed then to be for our neighbor's welfare. Luther put it well:

Now when you have Christ as the foundation and chief blessing of your salvation, then the other part follows: that you take him as your example, giving yourself in service to your neighbor just as you see that Christ has given himself for you. See, there faith and love move forward, God's commandment is fulfilled, and a person is happy and fearless to do and to suffer all things. Therefore make note of this, that Christ as a gift nourishes your faith and makes you a Christian. But Christ as an example exercises your works. These do not make you a Christian. Actually they come forth from you because you have already been made a Christian. As widely as a gift differs from an example, so widely does faith differ from works, for faith possesses nothing of its own, only the deeds and life of Christ. Works have something of your own in them, yet they should not belong to you but to your neighbor. (Martin Luther, "What to Look for and Expect in the Gospels," *Luther's Works* 35:120)

In medieval Christianity, suffering was seen as a way to participate in Christ's saving activity—one "offered up" one's suffering to add to that of Jesus and thus help in the process of salvation. The reformers proclaimed that Christ's work is complete and doesn't require our addition. But suffering plays a part in Christian life. It gives our faith a place to mature and it helps us better understand the suffering of others. The Samaritan, familiar with being rejected and scorned, is able to appreciate the situation of the beaten man. God, knowing human suffering in Christ, is able to come to us in our suffering. Suffering is a part of human life. We do not seek out suffering, but suffering, trials, and temptations can be good teachers.

Devotional Context

"What must I do to inherit eternal life?" is the question of the lawyer. All people ask such questions but perhaps in different ways: "How can I matter?" "What makes life worth living?" "How could anybody like me?" "What can I do to get along?" These questions touch something deep in our human need to feel worthwhile, loved, significant, or meaningful. The text allows participants to ask about the value of questioning and doubt in the life of faith. Luther observed that faith requires doubt as a fire requires fuel—take away the fuel and the fire dies.

The session speaks both of our reception of help from God and our freedom to help each other. We may tend to judge the strength of our faith by the feelings we have or the abilities we have to help others. But our trust isn't based on our abilities to be good helpers, but rather on God's promise of forgiveness.

SESSION SIX

Facilitator's Prayer

Dear God, open me to know that I am both the wounded person at the side of the road whom you heal and the one called to be a caregiver. Help me receive your mercy with joy and extend my mercy with love. Amen.

Gather (10-15 minutes)

Check-in

Take this time to connect or reconnect with the others in your group. Be ready to share new thoughts or insights about your last session. Also be ready to share any insights from homework or enrichment exercises.

Tip: Invite participants to think about times they have been helped and times they have given help as a way of entering the study of this session.

Pray

Compassionate God, you are with us all through our lives. You see our moments of triumph and joy as well as times of defeat and sadness. We ask you to help us rejoice in those times when joy is around us. We ask you to help us even to treasure those times of sorrow or loneliness, that we might learn tenderness and compassion for others from our own times of need. We pray this through Christ our neighbor. Amen.

Tip: One person prays the prayer. After the words *triumph and joy*, pause and encourage participants to name such times. After the words *defeat and sadness*, also pause to allow participants to name such times.

Focus Activity

Look at the Focus Image for the day. How would you describe the story that's behind the picture? Today's session text talks about unlikely helpers and surprising service.

- What are some examples of real life stories that would further illustrate the Focus Image?
- Have you ever helped or been helped by someone you considered to be an opponent. Describe the situation.

Tip: Have you ever heard of the real story of Sara Tucholsky, a softball player at Western Oregon University? In a game against Central Washington, she hit her first-ever home run but severely injured her right knee and could not circle and touch the bases. The referees ruled that nobody else on her team could run for her or help her. Mallory Holtmann and Liz Wallace, Central Washington players, volunteered to carry her from base to base and touch her foot on each base so that her run would count. They did this even though it cost them the game. For more coverage of this story go to blog.oregonlive.com/breakingnews/2008/04/the_best_tale_of_sportsmanship.html. You also might want to show the group the ESPN video at http://www.youtube.com/watch?v=jocw-oD2pgo.

Open Scripture (10-15 minutes)

Read the session text with each person taking a turn reading a verse. Begin with learners standing at the farthest distance apart in the room. After each verse, they take a step (or as many as will be needed) toward the meeting area, until by the end they are close together and ready to meet.

Have volunteers from the group act out the scenes as they are read (Jesus talking with the lawyer as well as the participants in Jesus' story).

Read Luke 10:25-37.

- Which of the characters in this text do you most identify with and which can you not understand?
- Why do you think the lawyer was testing Jesus?
- Is there anything strange about the answer to the question, "Who is my neighbor?"

Tip:
Open a fresh jar of aromatic ointment and pass it around while reading of the care given to the traveler. Perhaps some members might even apply the healing balm to themselves during the reading.

Join the Conversation (25-55 minutes)
Historical Context

Jewish "lawyers" (Luke 10:25) at the time of Christ were considered experts in Torah—the instructions of Hebrew scripture. While it may be the case that the lawyer in the text was an opponent of Jesus, it is more likely that he simply was carrying on the standard form of honoring a teacher or rabbi—by arguing. Even as Jesus is privately addressing his disciples, the lawyer asks his question. Without hesitation Jesus answers by asking another question; again, standard rabbinical practice. The issue may not have been showing who was right and who was wrong so much as being as clear and specific as possible with what the law requires.

1. Read Matthew 12:1-8 and Mark 10:17-22 and discuss the tactics and objectives of the questioners. How do they compare with Luke 10:25-29? What seems to be the difference between Jesus and his questioners?

Tip:
To illustrate the collaborative search for truth, have a set of puzzle pieces or toy building blocks and invite each person to add her or his piece until the puzzle or building is complete.

2. As you can see in Matthew 12:9-14 and Mark 10:23-27, Jesus often ended such question-and-answer sessions with a miracle, an illustration, or, in the case of Luke 10:30-37, a parable that drove his point home. What would you say is the central point of the parable of the good Samaritan? Write it below:

_____
_____
_____
_____
_____
_____

Tip:
Parables are not allegories. Instead of everything in the story meaning something else, parables are more like Aesop's Fables in that there is a moral to the story, a primary spiritual truth that the narrative sets up. Have learners try to refine their thoughts about the good Samaritan into a single sentence.

SESSION SIX

 Bonus Activity:
Have one of the participants read and summarize the history of the Samaritan community from a Bible dictionary or an encyclopedia. A good online source for Bible resources is Luther Seminary's "Enter the Bible" website. For an article on Samaria go to www.enterthebible.org/Bible.aspx?rid=1279.

Historically we know that those traveling between Jerusalem and Jericho took a mountainous road that was notorious for dangerous places. Jesus' hearers would have understood the peril. Priests and Levites taking that road were probably on official business and thus could not become ritually unclean by contact with blood. A Samaritan, to Jews, was both a heretic and a low-life. Not only would a good Judean not want help from a Samaritan, but would never expect to give or receive such help.

3. How would you contrast and compare the intentions of the lawyer with that of the Samaritan? Read Luke 17:11-19. In what ways does this parallel passage contrast the letter of the law with the spirit of love (Romans 13:8-10)?

Literary Context

Whether the question from the lawyer was an antagonistic test or a genuine debate, the form of this text is that of a confrontation. A problem or obstacle presents itself, Jesus responds, and there is an outcome that answers the problem. Preceding this confrontation, Luke records Jesus thanking the Father that it isn't the wise and intelligent but the "infants" who see God's grace (Luke 10:21-22). He also privately tells the disciples that they are seeing that which prophets and kings had wanted to see but didn't (Luke 10:23-24).

1. How does this literary foreshadowing set the confrontation with a legal expert and the commendation of the Samaritan in even greater contrast?

Bonus Activity:
Create a list of "outcast" groups in various places in local and national society (these could be racial, ethnic, economic, geographical, or just cliques).

Luke's Gospel highlights God's presence with and outreach to the alienated, the dispossessed, and the powerless. Here two "powerless" people meet each other—the man beaten and left near death and the Samaritan, away from his home, among people who despised him.

2. In Luke 10:33, Jesus speaks of the Samaritan being "moved with pity (compassion)" over the man's condition. Luke uses the same Greek word in Luke 7:13 and Luke 15:20. What do these texts tell us about the kind of emotion the Samaritan showed?

Close Encounters of the Jesus Kind Leader Guide

SESSION SIX

3. If the situation were reversed, what, according to Jeremiah 22:1-3, should have been the attitude of the Jews toward the Samaritan?

Lutheran Context

A very important aspect of Lutheran ethics is that we do not do good works in order to get to heaven. We do good for others because they need our help and it's the right thing to do. If we help a neighbor only to get to heaven, we're using that person, not serving him or her. The lawyer's question, then, illustrates the need he had to "justify himself" even if he was only reflecting the common spirituality.

1. A core Lutheran teaching is justification by grace through faith in Christ. How does Galatians 2:15-21 speak to the idea of one being able to justify himself or herself?

Lutheran theology is not against good works! In fact, good works are taken much more seriously because they are also a way of thanking God for God's grace. God frees us from working ourselves to the bone to get to heaven so that we might have energy to help our neighbors.

2. Read Galatians 5:1, 13-15. How do freedom and service fit together? Is that how we are used to defining *freedom*?

A common form of biblical prayer in Luther's time was called *lectio divina* ("sacred reading"). It involved *lectio, meditation, oratio,* and *contemplatio* (reading, meditation, praying, and comtemplation). To this Luther added *tentatio*—trials. Luther recognized that human life could not escape trials, but Luther also believed that trials could give us greater sympathy for our neighbors. The Samaritan knew what it was like to be rejected and could reach out to others on the wayside.

Bonus Activity:
Read Luke 7:13; Luke 15:20; and Luke 10:33 again, but substitute the phrase "moved in his guts" for the phrase "moved with pity." Discuss how this more literal translation of the Greek verb *splangchnizomai* (*splangk-NIZ-o-mai*) changed how you hear the text. Are there other idioms that retain this idea of deep passion being "gut wrenching"?

Tip:
How accurate is it to describe pity as a "gut feeling"? How can our bodily reactions help us understand what events mean for us?

Bonus Activity:
Role-play two scenarios: In the first, one person is in car trouble on the road and stops at a business to seek help; a second person is the owner of the business who does everything possible *not* to help. In the second, the same scenario, but the business owner is extravagant in the help offered. Discuss group reactions. Have we had similar experiences?

Tip:
You might want to read and discuss Luther's quote on the balance between faith and good works from the Session Overview.

Tip:
There is nothing inherently "good" or "noble" about suffering. It simply is a part of human life. Douglas John Hall points out that some suffering is simply part of creation (for example, Adam's loneliness for a companion in Genesis 2) and most suffering is counter to God's intention for creation (sickness, tragic death, warfare, for example). We do not seek it out, but faith equips us to encounter it (Douglas John Hall, *God and Human Suffering*, Minneapolis: Augsburg, 1986).

SESSION SIX

 Bonus Activity:
If time permits, lead the participants through a *lectio divina* exercise on one of today's passages. For more background on this practice, read the chapter "How Can the Bible Be Studied?" by Diane Jacobson in *Opening the Book of Faith* (Minneapolis: Augsburg Fortress, 2008).

 Bonus Activity:
Bring a number of magazines and newspapers. Ask participants to find headlines, pictures, or articles that illustrate either selfishness or service.

 Tip:
It will not be unusual if participants are uncomfortable speaking of personal trials or failure. Don't force such discussion; show sensitivity to those who choose to share.

 Bonus Activity:
Share the story of Tommy Dorsey's composition of "Precious Lord" and discuss how suffering can open us to God's grace. An Internet search on "Precious Lord, Take My Hand" will easily take you to a version of the story.

 Tip:
Pray the prayer antiphonally. That is, one person or one group reads the first half of each sentence ("As you have shown me mercy...") and the rest of the group prays the half following the comma ("... help me to be merciful.")

3. Share trials you have experienced that have made you more sensitive to the needs of others.

Devotional Context

The lawyer's question really does touch something deep in all of us. We may not ask what we need to do in order to inherit heaven, but all people of faith also have an element of doubt to their faith. Faith without doubt isn't really faith, anyway. We may wonder whether our faith is "strong enough" or if we are active enough in helping others or in our church.

1. In what ways can we find a soul mate in the lawyer and his question?

In contrast, the Samaritan in the parable reflects God's compassion and involvement with humankind—and not just humankind but also individual people. God answers our concerns about our own worthiness by rescuing, washing, anointing, healing, and then equipping us to serve others.

2. Read Psalm 139:7-12. What does it mean for our daily lives and self-regard that we cannot go or be any place where God isn't?

3. Write a prayer honestly stating areas in your life in which you experience trial or failure. Name each one and follow it up with the phrase "... and there you show me mercy, dear God." Pray that prayer each day for the next week.

Wrap-up

1. If there are any questions to explore further, write them on chart paper or a whiteboard.

2. Write a list of "My good works that belong to my neighbor" on the paper or whiteboard.

Pray

Dearest Lord, as you have shown me mercy, help me to be merciful. As you have given me grace, help me to be gracious. As you forgive me each day, help me to forgive. As you come to me and accept me, help me to accept others. As you heal me, send me into the world as a healer. As you look on me with compassion, help me to be compassionate. As you have given me all I am and have, help me to share myself with all. For Christ's sake. Amen.

Extending the Conversation (5 minutes)

Homework

1. Look over the six sessions you have spent time with. At the end of each write a summary statement of what you have learned. Revisit your list each week for the next month.

2. If you haven't yet, sign up for another unit of Book of Faith adult Bible studies.

3. Don't forget to keep going to www.bookoffaith.org. There you can continue the conversation and stay connected to one another and the Book of Faith initiative.

4. Do an Internet search for "good Samaritan" organizations in your community to see how you can help with their work.

Enrichment

1. Look in a local library or on the Internet for as many artistic representations of this parable as you can find. Choose one as your favorite and show it to another member of your group and discuss why you like it.

2. Read the story of Tommy Dorsey, composer of "Precious Lord." Especially note the setting in which he wrote that hymn.

3. Call a number of local congregations and organizations to ask them what the "entrance requirements" are to join their community. How do those requirements compare to what Luke has taught your group regarding the "estranged"?

For Further Reading

Available from augsburgfortress.org/store:

On Christian Liberty by Martin Luther (Minneapolis: Fortress Press, 2003). This is Luther's classic treatment of how the freedom of the gospel equips us to be servants of each other.

Opening the Book of Faith: Lutheran Insights for Bible Study by Diane L. Jacobson, Mark Allan Powell, and Stanley N. Olson (Minneapolis: Augsburg Fortress, 2008). A helpful introduction to the Book of Faith initiative, *Opening the Book of Faith* explores Lutheran perspectives on Scripture and applies these insights in practical ways.

SESSION SIX

Looking Ahead

1. Look over the six sessions you have spent time with. At the end of each write a summary statement of what you have learned. Revisit your list each week for the next month.

2. If you haven't already, prepare to facilitate another unit of Book of Faith adult Bible studies.

3. Encourage members of your group to think about their potential for leadership. Intentionally pray and work to develop involvement in Book of Faith small groups at your church.

4. Connecting with your synod's Book of Faith Advocate would be a great way to enhance this important ministry of biblical fluency.

www.ingramcontent.com/pod-product-compliance
Lightning Source LLC
Chambersburg PA
CBHW082247300426
44110CB00039B/2461